DUMONT'S LEXICON OF
SPICES

Origin • Taste • Use • Recipes

Anne Iburg

REBO
PUBLISHERS

© 2004 Rebo International b.v., Lisse, The Netherlands

This 2nd edition reprinted in 2006.

Text: Anne Iburg
Typesetting: AdAm Studio, Prague, The Czech Republic
Cover design: AdAm Studio, Prague, The Czech Republic

Translation: Magdalena Kaniová for Agentura Abandon, Prague, The Czech Republic
Proofreading: Emily Sands, Laura Grec

ISBN 90 366 1696 4

Contents

Introduction

Spices enrich our food and our lives. What would a burger be without pepper, pizza without oregano, mashed potatoes without nutmeg or plum jam without cinnamon? Tasteless, monotonous dishes! Spices are small and easily overlooked ingredients, but their role in culinary as well as cultural and even scientific history, is significant beyond their size. Spices have been fascinating people for centuries with their pungent aromas, delicate flavors, and curative properties, even as magical and aphrodisiacal powers have been, and still are, attributed to them. But everyone knows that important things sometimes come in very small packages!

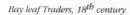

Bay leaf Traders, 18th century

HOW LONG HAVE PEOPLE USED SPICES?

The answer to this question is almost as difficult as the answer to the question of the chiken and the egg. People have probably been using spices ever since they began to cook, and it is that which distinguishes us from animals. We eat not only to appease our hunger and thirst, but to satisfy an aesthetic artistic desire as well. We need new flavors and new methods of preparation and delicious, as well as nourishing, dishes. Our ancestors discovered that certain leaves and fruits improved the taste of food. They spread leaves or berries onto meat before or after it was roasted in fire. They did not need pots to use spices, as some books suggest. However, the pot expanded the possibilities of using spices in cooking. Since the invention of the pot, spices could be stored and mixed.

The first evidence of spice usage by humans is from Mexico. The aboriginals of Mexico were already using chili to spice their food by 7,000 BC.

Pepper, a picture in a book, 17th century

SPICES IN ANCIENT TIMES

India is the cradle of spices in the Old World. About 5,000 years ago, a large trade network included China, India, Persia, Mesopotamia, and Egypt. Traces of anise, fenugreek, cardamom, cassia, caraway, dill, fennel and saffron have been found in the pyramids, which prove that they were used. At the time of the pharaohs in ancient Egypt, spices flavored the food of slaves as well as the rich. But spices did not, early in human history, have the purely aesthetic function they possess today. Adding spice to food was believed to protect people from epidemics and to mask the sour taste of spoiled food. Thus spices served both as ingredients and as a means to protect health.

The Ebers Papyrus, written in Egypt in 1500 BC, contains a collection of medical formulas. Today, it is housed in a university library in Leipzig. The lengthy paper contained information about more than 700 natural products. Scilla was used for anasarca, radish as a means to heal pectoral diseases, and garlic and onion were natural "antibiotics."

Herbal medicine in ancient Greece experienced its heyday during the time of Hippocrates (460 – 370 BC). He described, among other things, more than 230 medicinal herbs in his textbook "Corpus Hippocraticum." Hippocrates and his supporters, the so-called Asclepiads, worshipped Asclepius, the god of medicine and the son of Apollo in Greek mythology, as one of their ancestors. Hippocrates, already as a child, was taught by his father Herakleidas, according to their family tradition, about the effects and use of medicinal herbs. During his travels around Asia Minor and Greece, he practiced and developed his "medicinal arts" as a wandering doctor. Popular, respected and generally adored, he returned to Cos in order to manage his medical practice, write and teach medicine in his own school.

Hippocrates

Herbal medicine was widespread in ancient Rome as well. They were inspired in great part by the Greeks. We know that the Romans used dill, caraway, mustard, coriander, wild celery, garlic, thyme, marjoram, savory, parsley, anise, fennel, sesame, and poppy seeds when they cooked. Pepper was imported around the time of the birth of Christ. It was used by the richest Romans as a spice and even developed into an independent currency.

Many spices were carried to Central Europe by Roman legionaries. Some spices survived Roman occupation of the Rhine, Galicia or the British island of "Britannica" and are still used today.

TRADE ROUTES TO EUROPE

Spices were transported over old caravan routes from China across Asia to Europe for hundreds of years. We know that there were three main routes. The Silk Road is the best known of these trade routes. The exact route is no longer known today, but trade centers that were stops on the ancient trading routes still exist. After discovering a sea route to Europe around 100 AD, merchants sailed to South Africa and India and brought many spices to Europe to make perfumes, cosmetic's and medicine. However, the sea route was forgotten at the time of the decline of the Roman Empire and the Silk Road remained the most important way to exchange goods and exchange knowledge between Western Europe, the Orient and northern Africa.

Merchants kept a tight grip on trading along the ancient Silk Road even into the early Middle Ages. They travelled from Samarkand eastwards, reaching the colonies of East Turkestan, Mongolia and China. They transported goods from the east to the west and in the opposite direction as well – partially on the backs of their camels and partially on their own backs as well. Dealing with currency was often impossible so they exchanged goods: silk for spices, spices for lapis

lazuli, jade and silver jewelry, jewelry for sable and other furs, furs for woolen covers, covers for luxury glassware and so on. In this way, oriental spices came to Europe.

HERBAL GARDEN IN THE MIDDLE AGES'S

Work in a walled-in city garden,
a picture in a book, 15th century

In 802, Charles the Great published "Capitulare de villis et curtis imperialibus," a collection of regulations for cloisters, homesteads and granges in his domain. The law regulated exactly which spices and plants could be grown by monks, dukes and barons, and dictated which plants were useful to men and animals as food, spices, medicinal herbs or insect repellents. Local spices included wild garlic, tarragon, savory, and watercress as well as Mediterranean plants like rosemary, coriander and sage. Plants from more distant lands were brought to northern and Central Europe in the form of seeds, seedlings or runners. Many herbs are multifunctional: they spice and heal (like mint and caraway) or spice and preserve (like dill).

The abbess Hildegard von Bingen (1098–1179 AD) lived during the time of Barbarossa. She describes in minute detail the healing effects and powers of individual plants in her manuscripts. She describes exactly what plant is needed, which dose is necessary and which part of the plant is used.

Hildegard von Bingen

Herbs were used to stop bleeding, for colds, coughs and rhinitis, for stomach and intestinal disorders, skin eczema and ulcers, sprains, fractures, dysmenorrhea and even to induce abortions. Some herbs were perspiratory and diuretic. There was even an herb to heal insect and snakebites as well as to repel flees, lice and bedbugs.

THE CRUSADES – WARS FOR HERBS IN THE MIDDLE AGES

The Arabs dominated the exchange of goods between Asia and Europe until the Crusades owing to the supremacy of Islam. The Arabic empires of Abbasids and Fatimids, with their cities and principal trading centers of Byzantium, Alexandria and Cairo, were vital links in the exchange of goods (including spices) between the Orient and the Occident. The adventures of a merchant and navigator called Sindbad were recounted in Arab cafés.

The demand for spices increased in the West during the Crusades. As a consequence of conquering what is today Syria and Palestine, the Christians assumed control of the most significant trade regions between the West and the East. The Europeans founded Crusade States all over the Mediterranean region and in the Levant in particular. Since they lacked a fleet of their own, they used the ships of northern Italian merchants.

Under the reign of Genghis Khan in the 13th century, the Mongolians conquered a large empire which extended from the China Sea to the Mediterranean. The tolerance of the Mongolians allowed Italian merchants to travel directly to the original sources of the spices. Marco Polo (1254–1324) only returned to his home in Venice after twenty-four years of traveling the Silk Road to China.

Spice Merchants in the Market in Sanaa, Yemen

VENICE AND THE MONOPOLY OF THE ITALIANS

Ippolito Caffi, Piazza San Marco, Venice, 1858

The Crusades were ideal for the Venetians because they allowed them to circumvent the Arab merchants, via Christian strongholds in Asia, and buy spices at advantageous prices. The Arabs from Levant and the Venetians shared the European spice market. The Arabs were oriental spice merchants who brought spices to the Venetians from Asia. Their prices were high, but the Venetians still always tried to resell the goods at the highest possible prices. Therefore, the profit margins for these spice merchants were enormous. The price of a spice could increase a hundred times during its journey from Calcutta to Venice in the 14th century. One pound of saffron cost as much as a horse, a pound of ginger cost as much as a sheep, and pepper was partially balanced with gold. Spices were emblems of wealth: they were offered as gifts to rulers or requested as ransom. For over 400 hundred years, Venice, Genoa and Pisa owed their wealth to the spice trade.

During the Middle Ages, adulterating spices was common because demand was high and everybody wanted to make the highest profit possible. The authorities reacted harshly. In Nuremberg, a counterfeiter of spices was burnt alive together with his goods. But harsh punishments failed to deter counterfeiters reaping the benefits of the high demand for spices.

After the Mongolians lost their control over China and the advancing Ming dynasty strengthened, direct trade between Europe and China was interrupted. The spice merchants did business with traders from Beirut, Tripoli and Alexandria. The sailing experience of early modern times encouraged the southerners to embark on risky sailing expeditions: from the Mediterranean through the Straits of Gibraltar, they explored the coasts of Portugal, northern Spain and France as well as central and northern Europe. Antwerp, Bruges and London became important, new centers for spice trading.

THE PORTUGUESE

The bold Portuguese sailed south along the African coast, bringing African spices to the West for the first time. After Vasco da Gama, a Portuguese navigator, returned from India in 1499 with full ships, Italian domination collapsed. The price of spices in Europe were now dictated in Lisbon. Pepper, cloves, ginger, cinnamon and nutmeg were among the most important trade goods. Imported cinnamon came from Ceylon, i. e. Sri Lanka nowadays. The Portuguese established a lucrative monopoly in the trade in cinnamon,

Ludolf Backhuysen, Fleet of the Dutch India Company, 1675

which financed their expensive expeditions of exploration.

The well-known wealth of the Fugger was initially based, among other things, on trade in spices. A mid-16th century legend says that the merchant Anton Fugger burnt Charles V's debenture notes before the eyes of the Emperor in a hearth made of valuable cinnamon sticks.

Paprika and Pimento – Discovered by the Spaniards

The Spaniards as well as the Portuguese invested much money in the sailing business. Isabella I and Ferdinand II of Spain equipped Christopher Columbus, a Genoese navigator, with three ships to enable him to execute his plan to find a sea route to India by sailing westwards. Although Columbus never arrived in India, he did discover the New World, America. America proved to have a wealth of new and exciting spices as well as other goods. Exploration, funded by the Spanish rulers, expanded the knowledge of spices in Europe.

The Dutch East Indian Company accompanied Columbus on his second discovery sail. They brought new spices back to Europe with them in about 1494. Pimento trees bore no fruit in their new country and vanilla could not be grown in Europe. However, paprika and chili plants conquered the Old World. At the beginning, paprika was regarded as a species of pepper and paprika plants, so-called Spanish pepper, were thought of as exotic foliage plants. Almost 100 years later, paprika started to be grown in Spain and soon spread all over Europe. It found a new home in Hungary and became a Hungarian national spice. Today, chili peppers are grown all over the world.

Besides Columbus, the Spaniards also engaged Fernand Magellan, a Portuguese explorer. He was the first to sail around the globe. However, he did not survive the sail and only one single ship in his fleet returned. But it was so loaded with spices and other goods that the profits from the goods on board outbalanced the costs of the journey. After the Spaniards and the Portuguese agreed to share the trade in spices – Spain trading with the West and Portugal with the East – another trade nation set sail in the direction of the Far East to capture its share of the wealth of spices: the Dutch triumphantly entered in the world of spices.

Work on a Plantation, India, 18th century

COLONIES BRING WEALTH TO EUROPE

The ruthless exploitation of the indigenous peoples and of the mineral resources of the New World constitutes a sad chapter in the history of spices. The colonial domination definitively ended, along with the monopoly in spices, only after World War II in 1945, several centuries later.

The Dutch East India Company, a powerful trading company and the first joint-stock enterprise, conquered the trade in nutmeg and cloves. They took Moluccas from the Portuguese and benefited from Portugal's monopoly in the clove and nutmeg trade: the Dutch East India Company sold nutmeg in Europe at a 200 percent surcharge. The Dutch defended these profits ferociously: nutmeg as well as clove trees could be grown only on two Moluccas Isles, Ambon and Banda. All other trees were destroyed. Whoever planted nutmeg or clove trees without official permission was executed and whoever stole a nut had his hand cut off. Eventually, the Dutch relaxed such Draconian measures. In about 1770, the French managed to steal a few small nutmeg trees and clove seedlings from the Moluccas and plant them in their own colonies on Madagascar, Mauritius and Reunion. Thus the monopoly over both spices was terminated forever.

Drogist, 17th century

The Dutch East India Company went bankrupt in 1780 and the English blocked Dutch ships in East India.

London became the most important center for the spice trade in Sri Lanka and India and cinnamon brought high profits to English merchants.

SPICES AND HERBS FALL INTO OBLIVION

We cannot explain exactly why spices and herbs went out of fashion in the 19th century. The demand for spices dropped while other products, such as cocoa, coffee and sugar, became important to the diets of rich Europeans. Seasoning dishes lavishly went out of style and many herbs fell into oblivion. New foods like potatoes, rice, tomatoes and brussels sprouts became popular ingredients. Spices experienced their comeback only after World War II when they began to be sold in boxes and jars, attracting the interest of modern housewives. Because people enjoyed traveling and discovering other cultures in the second half of the 20th century, fascination with exotic cuisines and spices was revived again.

House of the Dutch East India Company, London, 17th century

SPICES IN COOKING

Spices and dried herbs should preferentially "sleep" in your kitchen. In other words, storing spices in decorative, non-lightproof jars in not suitable at all. They grow pale with exposure to light, losing both their color and aroma. Even though it is convenient to store spices directly next to your stove, excess heat and humidity also deteriorates their flavor. Ideally spices and dried herbs should be stored in air-tight containers in dark, cool, dry places.

Spices and herbs only like "socializing" conditionally. You should not store more than one type of spice in the same container at the same time because each spice, while exuding fragrant and aromatic substances, also easily absorbs other smells fast.

Even if you store your spices perfectly, you should check the aromas of your stock from time to time. You can tell a spice is spoiled because it simply loses its aroma and taste.

THE SPICE LEXICON

The following comments should help you to become familiar with the structure of the Spice Lexicon:

The herbs are listed alphabetically according to their botanical names. Their English name is noted below. Any other colloquial name is included under "Synonyms."

The boxes in the side column refer you to the most important attributes of each plant. The symbols mean the following:

Use:	*Edible part:*	*Origin:*
✗ Spice used in cooking	✿ Blossom	Africa
🅰 Medicinal	🍐 Fruit	America
	🌿 Leaves	Asia
	🌾 Herbaceous stems, Bark	Europe
	♦ Root, Bulb	

Properties:

! Some of the herbs listed can cause allergies in sensitive persons or miscarriage in pregnant women. Some are poisonous depending on the dosage. The risk depends mainly on the dosage, the part of the plant used and the preparation of the plant prior to use.

Therefore, pay appropriate attention to the comments on the last page of each citation. It is better not to use the spice if you have any doubts.

Allium sativum
Garlic

Origin:

Asia

Edible part:

Use:

FAMILY: *Alliaceae*

SYNONYMS: Clown's treacle

FORMS OF USE: Bulb, fresh, whole, or in the form of a paste, dried and ground

ORIGIN: Garlic is probably native to western Asia. However, it is grown in temperate and subtropical climate's in all parts of the world today. Garlic remains a common flavor in most cuisines and a staple of the average kitchen's spice closet.

PROPERTIES: Garlic is a plant about 28 inches high. It consists of one egg-shaped central bulb and about 12 side bulbs usually called "cloves." A tubular herbaceous stem and thin long leaves grow from the central bulb. Reddish-white blossoms bloom at the turn of July and August and form a globular fault umbel. Garlic contains many sulfur compounds. Allicine (diallyl disulfide oxide), generated from alliine when a clove is cut, is valued for its taste.

RELATED SPECIES: Botanically, garlic is related to other members of the Alliaceae family, such as chives, wild garlic and onion.

MYTHOLOGY: The Romans regarded garlic as an aphrodisiac. Eating its cloves was supposed to increase potency in men. According to certain eastern European legends, eating garlic protects people from the bites of bloodthirsty vampires.

MEDICINAL USE: Already around 1500 BC, garlic was used in various medicinal formulas and the ancient Greeks in particular used it to cure many diseases. During the Middle Ages, doctors prescribed garlic for bone fractures and freckles. Garlic was valued for its healing effects until today. However, it does have an antiseptic effect and releases mucus. Garlic broth can be used externally for sore throats

or inflamed swellings as well as a drink to soothe coryza and bronchitis.

If used regularly, the sulfur compounds of garlic should help poor blood circulation.

TIPS FOR COOKING

You can recognize fresh garlic by its hard white cloves covered with a dry peel. When buying garlic, push carefully on the bulb.

Maybe you wonder why some bulbs are rose and others are white. The difference in taste is insignificant. Gourmet cooks usually prefer rose colored garlic.

Garlic paste tastes very similar to bulbs. Use salt or powder only if you want to season something quickly.

Before you start peeling and cutting garlic, moisten your hands and the cutting board - they will release their smell faster.

Garlic develops its full aroma only when pressed through a garlic press or sliced with a knife. When garlic is roasted in oil or cooked, it loses its piquancy.

IN THE KITCHEN

AROMA:
Garlic has a slightly savory, slightly sweetish taste. It smells like sulfur and therefore it is peculiarly penetrating.

USE:
Garlic is the universal spice for all spicy dishes. It plays a big role in Mediterranean and Asian cuisines. Garlic is very dominant in tapas, antipastos or mezzos. It goes well with meat and fish, soufflés and soups. Its aroma contributes to some salad dressings and dips.

HIDDEN USE:
Whether mixed into Italian pesto, Asian curry, pasta or Indian spice dishes, many cooks consider garlic an essential ingredient.

BUYING/STORING:
Garlic is available all year round. In spring, young garlic can be eaten whole as a vegetable. If it is stored in a dark, dry place, it will last for several months. Garlic paste, both in a jar and in a tube, should be stored in a refrigerator once opened. Garlic powder as well as salt should be firmly closed and stored in a dark place.

Allium tuberosum
Chinese chives

FAMILY: *Alliaceae*

SYNONYMS: Oriental garlic

FORMS OF USE: Leaves, herbaceous stems and blossoms

ORIGIN: Chinese chives have been grown in Asia for hundreds of years.

PROPERTIES: A Chinese chive is a cross-breed of garlic and chives. A perennial plant which grows up to 20 in (50 cm) high, it resembles very thick chives in appearance, but is slightly bigger.

RELATED SPECIES: Its closest botanical relatives are chives and garlic. Onion, leek and wild garlic belong among its more distant relatives.

MEDICINAL USE: Chinese chives are appreciated in Chinese medicine for their ability to stimulate digestion.

IN THE KITCHEN

AROMA:
Chinese chives taste and smell like chives with a hint of garlic.

USE:
Chinese chives are common in Asian cuisine, as ingredients in salads, soups and stews as well as egg dishes.

BUYING/STORING:
Chinese chives are available in Asian stores all year round. They should be wrapped in a moist towel and stored in a freezer bag in the vegetable compartment of a refridgerator for 1 – 3 days.

TIPS FOR COOKING:
You can tell Chinese chives are fresh if the buds are closed. Always add Chinese chives last because they lose their aroma when cooked for a long time.
Chinese chives should be sliced with scissors instead of with a knife.
If you want to store Chinese chives for a longer time, freeze them sliced with little water to form ice cubes.
Chinese chives lose their aroma if they dry out.

Allium ursinum
Wild garlic

Origin:
Europe, Asia

Edible part:

Use:
✗ ♉

Property:
❗

FAMILY: *Alliaceae*

SYNONYMS: Ransoms, bear's garlic, buckrams, gipsy onion, hog's garlic

FORMS OF USE: Leaves, fresh

ORIGIN: Wild garlic grows in Europe and northern Asia in humid, humus-rich soils, shaded in deciduous and bottomland forests.

PROPERTIES: Wild garlic sprouts in March alongside the first snowdrops and the first green shoots of nettle. At the end of June, when its seeds are ripe and its lanceolate leaves draw in, the 8 – 20 inch plants terminate their annual cycle. The leaf shape is reminiscent of the leaves of lilies-of-the-valley. The leaves of wild garlic contain a high concentration of sulfur, magnesium, manganese and iron compounds. Substances containing sulfur are proteins like glutathione and cysteine. Some sulfur-containing compounds are released when the leaves are cut or ground, explaining the fact that the smell of wild garlic is similar

IN THE KITCHEN

AROMA:
Wild garlic tastes fresh and resembles garlic. Its smell is slightly similar to the smell of sulfur.

USE:
You can certainly find wild garlic in many of your grandmother's recipes. Wild garlic is usually minced and added to butter, cottage cheese, yogurt or cream soups. When cut into fine strips, it is suitable for spring salads.

BUYING/STORING:
You can buy wild garlic in the marketplace from March to May. Wrap it in a moist towel and store it in a freezer bag in the vegetable compartment of a refridgerator for 1 – 3 days.

TIPS FOR COOKING:
Wild garlic should not be cooked because it loses its aroma. When you want to stock up on wild garlic, you should mince it, mix it with a little water and freeze it into ice cubes.

IMPORTANT WARNING:

If you want to pick wild garlic yourself in spring, be careful not to confuse it with the poisonous leaves of lilies-of-the-valley. If the leaves exude a garlic-like fragrance, you know that you have picked the correct herb.

Alpinia galanga
Galangal

Origin:
Asia

Edible part:
◊

Use:
✕ 🐀

Property:
❗

FAMILY: Ginger (*Zingiberaceae*)

SYNONYMS:

FORMS OF USE: Root, fresh, dried ground into powder or pickled

ORIGIN: Galangal is native to the tropics, specifically Indonesia. The plant is grown in southeast Asia, Thailand, Malaysia and Indonesia. But people in Western countries are also familiar with it.

PROPERTIES: Galangal is a perennial plant. It has creeping cylindrical, mostly bent rhizomes (roots). The roots have characteristic, yellowish-white blossoms, which are arranged decoratively around the rhizomes. Pink or reddish side sprouts grow from the rhizomes. After the roots are harvested, they are cut into 4 – 8 inch pieces one inch thick. The rhizome contains essential oils and resin (galangol, alpinol), which cause its very bitter taste.

RELATED SPECIES: Galangal is closely related to lesser galangal (*Alpinia officinarum*). The lesser, and spicier, galangal is probably native to southern China. Fresh galangal is not readily available.

MYTHOLOGY: Galangal was regarded as a "magic means" in the area of its origin for a long time. Substances contained in it were believed to have euphoriant and aphrodisiac properties.

MEDICINAL USE: The healing power of galangal was celebrated outside of Asia. Doctor Mattioli wrote in the 16th century: "Galangal refreshes breath, promotes digestion and removes flatulence." Paracelsus had a similar opinion. Hildegard von Bingen, a Benedictine abbess, describes galangal as a means of healing heart diseases: "Who suffers from heart problems and who is endangered by an attack of heart weakness should eat a sufficient amount of galangal immediately and his condition will improve."

A concoction made from galangal powder helps to relieve itchy, irritated skin. Galangal is contained in the herbal medicine "Schwedenbitter." It is used to ease cramps in angina pectoris.

HAVE YOU TASTED IT?

SHRIMP SKEWERS IN GALANGAL SAUCE

Peel a piece of galangal about 1 in long and mince. Rinse about 18 shrimp in cold water and dry. Pierce 3 shrimp with a wooden skewer and sprinkle a little lemon juice over them. Melt 1 tablespoon of margarine in a pan. Fry the galangal with 2 minced chili peppers, a pinch of cumin and 2 minced curry leaves. Add 1 cup coconut milk and simmer for about 10 minutes. Put the skewered shrimps in the coconut milk and simmer for about 5 minutes.

IN THE KITCHEN

AROMA:
The taste of galangal resembles that of ginger, but it is finer. It smells like citrus fruit and pine.

USE:
Galangal is a basic element of Asian cuisine. It is suitable for spicy stews and curry dishes, it goes well with poultry and lamb as well as fish and seafood.

BUYING/STORING:
Galangal is available in Asian specialty stores in western countries. Roots stay fresh for 2 - 3 weeks if stored in the vegetable compartment of a refridgerator wrapped in a freezer bag to protect from drying. Galangal powder stored in an airtight container in a cool, dark place lasts for months.

TIPS FOR COOKING:
Fresh galangal is peeled as ginger and cut, grated or thinly sliced.
Fibrous galangal roots can be dried as well. For this purpose, peeled roots are cut into thin slices. Dunk dried galangal roots in a little water for 1 - 2 hours before using them.
If no fresh galangal is available, you can substitute fresh ginger.

> **IMPORTANT WARNING:**
>
> **Galangal promotes menses and can cause earlier menses or miscarriage.**

Apium graveolens
Wild celery

Origin:

Europe

Edible part:

Use:
✕ ♨

FAMILY: Carrot (*Apiaceae*)

SYNONYMS: Celeriac, apio, turnip-rooted celery

FORMS OF USE: Seeds, whole or ground, leaves, herbaceous stem and tuber

ORIGIN: Celery is of European origin and its wild form flourishes in alkalin and humid, calcic regions.

PROPERTIES: Celery was used in cooking earlier than tuberous or striped vegetables. However, it fell into oblivion. It has very tiny, brown, slightly wrinkled fruits. The plant, its wild form in particular, slightly resembles Italian parsley. Its seeds are rich in terpenes, which cause its bitter taste.

MEDICINAL USE: Wild celery seeds can alleviate urinary bladder diseases and young celery spouts can promote the digestion of heavy dishes.

IN THE KITCHEN

AROMA:
The taste of wild celery seeds is similar to the taste of tuber and striped celery, but much more bitter and pungent.

USE:
Wild celery seeds go mainly with vegetable and fish dishes. Soups and stews as well as relishes and pickles are often spiced with wild celery seeds. It can be used to enhance bread and savory baked goods as well. Celery salt contains both the leaves and ground seeds of celery.

BUYING/STORING:
Wild celery seeds are available in spice stores. Wild celery seeds and powder should be stored in airproof containers in a cool, dark place to preserve their aroma longer.

TIPS FOR COOKING:
To best release their aroma, wild celery seeds should be slightly crushed before use. Use the seeds in moderation, or the dish will have a bitter taste.

Armoracia rusticana
Horseradish

Origin:

Europe

Edible part:

Use:

Property:

!

FAMILY: Mustard (*Brassicaceae*)

SYNONYMS: Horse radish, red cole, cran, cranson, meredic, rabano picante

FORMS OF USE: Root, fresh, whole and grated, as a paste, dried, as powder or in flakes, ground, in powder or pickled

ORIGIN: Horseradish is native to eastern and southern Europe. The wild form of this plant grows in the steppes of eastern Russia and Ukraine. It is cultivated all over Europe, Asia and North America.

PROPERTIES: Horseradish is a perennial plant up to 4 feet high. The horseradish herbaceous stems - rhizomes - are 12 – 16 inches, exceptionally even up to 24 inches), long and 2 – 2½ long inches thick. The end of the root has side sprouts, which are removed by horseradish growers. It is very hard manual work to dig out and replant the main root twice during its growth time. Horseradish contains two times more vitamin C than lemon.

It is rich in vitamins B1, B2 and B6 as well as in mineral substances like potassium, magnesium and iron. Essential oils are responsible for its distinctive taste.

RELATED SPECIES: Horseradish is related to vegetable radish. Daikon radish, used mainly in Asian cuisine, belongs to the family of winter radish. Wasabi, sometimes called green horseradish, is not related.

MYTHOLOGY: Magic powers are attributed to horseradish. It increases stamina.

MEDICINAL USE: Horseradish aids immunity and insulates against the cold. It promotes digestion and blood circulation and decreases blood pressure. Used externally, it soothes rheumatism, arthritis, sciatica and insect bites. It relieves headache and other light strains as well.

Schamel, a German family undertaking, has been exporting horseradish roots worldwide in big wooden barrels since 1846. At the beginning of the 20th century, Johann Jakob Schamel came up with the idea to sell fresh-grated horseradish in small jars, saving housewives the tedious bother of grating the acrid sharp roots.

IN THE KITCHEN

AROMA:
Its taste is sharp and acrid. Fresh-grated horseradish fills the eyes with tears. Its smell is very acrid.

USE:
Horseradish is an essential spice in Bavarian and Austrian cuisines. Horseradish is added to beef dishes and goes well with hearty stews and soups.

BUYING/STORING:
Horseradish roots should be used fresh immediately after digging. They should remain whole if stored. The white flesh should not be grayish. The root cannot have more than two heads and should weigh at least 6 oz. Fresh horseradish is available from October to March. You can store it in a cold cellar or in the refridgerator. You should use bottled horseradish during the rest of the year. Horseradish powder and flakes are rarely available.

TIPS FOR COOKING:
Horseradish powder and flakes must be mixed with water. The potency of horseradish roots peaks at harvest time in the fall and then gradually decreases. Pay attention to this fact when cooking with fresh horseradish.

IMPORTANT WARNING:

The pungent spice can irritate skin and mucous membranes. In sensitive people, it can also irritate the stomach, bowels and kidneys.

Artemisia dracunculus
Tarragon

Origin:

Asia

Edible part:

Use:

FAMILY: Aster (*Asteraceae*)

SYNONYMS: Estragon, French tarragon, green sagewort, silky wormwood, false estragon

FORMS OF USE: Leaves and young sprouts, fresh and dried, crushed and ground

ORIGIN: Tarragon is probably native to central Asia, specifically Siberia. It has been familiar in Europe since the Middle Ages and is now cultivated all over the Northern Hemisphere.

PROPERTIES: Tarragon is a 4 ft high perennial herb with many branches. It has many stemless, round or slightly toothed and slightly lanceolate leaves. Tarragon is very seldom seen in bloom: it has little yellow blossoms forming a panicle.

RELATED SPECIES: French tarragon (*Artemisia redowskii*) is its closest relative and is a spice as well. However, its taste is more bitter and therefore it is less popular.

MYTHOLOGY: The translation of the word "dracunculus" refers to its mythological significance: "little dragon." People in the Middle Ages were convinced that tarragon functioned as an antibody against poisonous animal bites.

MEDICINAL USE: The tea of tarragon blossoms and leaves promotes and supports kidney functions.

Have you ever tasted it?

Cherry tomatoes in tarragon vinegar

Spike 2 lbs cherry tomatoes with a toothpick. Peel 4 garlic cloves. Pour 8 cups white wine vinegar into a big pot; add 3 twigs of tarragon, the garlic cloves and 1 teaspoon pimento grains. Simmer the liquid for about 10 minutes. Cool down and strain the vinegar from the other ingredients. Divide the tomatoes into four jam jars (about 4 cups per jar), and pour the vinegar into each jar up to about 1 inch below the rim. Close the jars and leave in the refridge-ration for a few days. The pickled tomatoes should last for about 8 weeks in a cool place.

FINES HERBES

Did you know that tarragon is, next to parsley, chives and chervil, one of the *"Fines Herbes,"* a classic French herb mix? This mix is available fresh or dried. The herbs are always contained in the same proportions in the mix. It is better to use fresh herbs. Omelets and scrambled eggs, cream soups, fresh cheese, cottage cheese and butter are often seasoned with *"Fines Herbes."*

TARRAGON MUSTARD

Tarragon mustard is definitely the most popular aromatized herbal mustard. It is native to France. The taste of this mustard is very fine and goes well in salad dressing or with light, fine dishes like stewed fish.

Have you ever tasted it?

Tarragon vinegar

Put about 5 twigs of tarragon into a sterilized 3 cup bottle. Boil white wine vinegar and pour into the bottle so that the twigs are completely covered with the liquid. Close the bottle with a cork and leave in the sun for up to 3 weeks. Then strain off the vinegar and use to season lettuce salads. It is delicious.

Tarragon butter

Wash, dry and mince 1 bundle of tarragon with a heavy knife. Mix the tarragon with a pinch of salt and 5 oz softened butter. This butter goes well with fish dishes and may be frozen without problems. The aroma is preserved nicely in the butter fat.

IN THE KITCHEN

AROMA:
Tarragon has a sweetly pungent, slightly peppery aroma with the flavor of anise.

USE:
Tarragon is added to many classic sauces like béarnaise or tartar sauce. It goes well mainly with light poultry dishes, stewed fish and simple egg dishes. This herb is used in salad dressings and mustard sauces very often as well.

BUYING/STORING:
It is always better to buy fresh tarragon because its aroma is most intense. Wrap it in a moist towel and store it in a freezer bag in the vegetable compartment of the refridgerator for 2 – 3 days. If you must use dried tarragon, buy only small quantities and store it in airproof containers in a dark, cool place.

TIPS FOR COOKING:
The herbaceous stems of tarragon can be cooked if preparing broths or stews. However, the leaves should not be cooked for a long time or they will lose their aroma.
Tarragon goes well with homemade condiments. You can also use it to enchance mustard.

Artemisia vulgaris
Wormwood

Origin:

Asia

Edible part:

Use:

✗ ♌

FAMILY: Aster (*Asteraceae*)

SYNONYMS: Common mugwort, mugwort, fellon-herb

FORMS OF USE: Leaves, fresh and dried, ground and crushed

ORIGIN: Wormwood is native to the temperate zone of Asia, but it has been used all over Europe and North America for a long time. It is cultivated in the Balkans, Germany and France.

PROPERTIES: Wormwood is a perennial plant and grows up to 6 feet high. Its herbaceous stems are angular and bluish-red. The leaves are dark green on the top and white and velvety underneath. Its small dark yellow blossom heads bloom in late summer. Only the leaves of its upper part are used as a spice, not the ones growing in the lower part. The leaves must be harvested before the plant starts blooming or they will become too bitter.

RELATED SPECIES: Wormwood is closely related to absinthe (Artemisia absinthium). Both species contain a high proportion of bitter substances, particularly when blooming.

MYTHOLOGY: This herb was regarded in the Middle Ages as a very effective means against and for magic. Wormwood was a part of many magic potions. It was supposed to relieve dysmenorrhea and strengthen people suffering from pulmonary tuberculosis. Pliny recommended that people about to set off on a long journey put wormwood in their shoes.

Wormwood picked during on the summer solstice is special. If you dig up the roots of the herb during the night of June 24th, you will find little pieces of coal. Worn as amulets, they are supposed to relieve fever and epilepsy. It is said as well that they protect from burns, plague and strokes of lightening.

The Germans wore wormwood picked on Midsummer Night attached to their belts next to their loins to protect their bodies from disease.

MEDICINAL USE: Wormwood eases stomach problems and has spasmolytic, diuretic, antibacterial and antifungicide properties. It promotes digestion and is therefore appropriate in recipes containing fat.

HAVE YOU EVER TASTED IT?

EEL IN A CRUNCHY JACKET
Skin an eel of about 2 lbs, disembowel, and cut in about 3 inch pieces. Wash and dry them well. Spice with celery salt and pepper. Wash a few twigs of wormwood, dill and Italian parsley and chop very finely. Mix 2 egg yolks, salt, pepper and ⅛ cup flour, then add about ⅛ cup light beer until you get a thick dough. Whip 2 egg whites and add to the dough. Dip the pieces of eel in the herbal mix and in the batter and fry in a deep fryer for about 5 minutes until crunchy and golden.

IN THE KITCHEN

AROMA:
The taste of wormwood is slightly bitter and acrid. Its smell resembles a mix of mint and juniper.

USE:
Wormwood goes well with fatty goose, duck, pork or lamb roasts. It makes cabbage dishes more digestible and is used as a spice for fatty eel dishes.

BUYING/STORING:
Wormwood is mainly available dried. It can be stored in an air-proof container in a dark and dry place. Fresh wormwood is available in marketplaces only in late summer. If wrapped in a freezer bag and stored in the vegetable compartment of the refridgerator, it remains fresh for 2 – 3 days.

TIPS FOR COOKING:
Always add wormwood to dishes at the beginning of their preparation because it develops its aroma only after being heated.
You can freeze fresh, minced wormwood.
Wormwood is a maverick. It does not combine well with other spices because its pungent, bitter taste dominates other aromas.

Bixa orellana
Annatto

FAMILY: Bixaceae

SYNONYMS: Urucum, achiote, urucu

FORMS OF USE: Seeds, dried, whole and ground

ORIGIN: The bush is native to South America. It is grown in the Caribbean, Mexico and in the Philippines as well.

PROPERTIES: The bush grows up to 6 feet high. Its pink blossoms resemble roses. The seeds are contained in heart-shaped shells with thorns resembling sweet chestnuts.

IN THE KITCHEN

AROMA:
Annatto has a light floral odor. Fresh annatto seeds are peppery. However, they lose their aroma fast if dried.

USE:
Annatto is used mainly in Caribbean and Latin American cuisines. Besides being used as a spice, it gives food an orange color. British cheddar is colored with annatto as well.

BUYING/STORING:
Annatto is available only in special spice stores. Its seeds can be stored for very long periods of time in air-proof closed containers stored in a dark place. The seeds should be brick red, not brownish.

TIPS FOR COOKING:
The best way to process the seeds is to make oil of them. Put the seeds into a little hot oil and when the oil turns orange, cool it and remove the seeds. The mixture stored in a dark bottle lasts as long as the oil.

Capparis spinosa
Caper

Origin:

Europe

Edible part:

Use:

FAMILY: Capparaceae

SYNONYMS: Common caper, bush capers

FORMS OF USE: Blossom buds, fresh, in a brine, oil or vinaigrette

ORIGIN: The caper bush is common thronghorn the entire Mediterranean region. The ancient Egyptians were familiar with it. The best capers are grown in Marseille, Nice and on the Lipari Islands, north of Sicily.

PROPERTIES: The thorny caper bush grows about 3 feet high. Its leaves are round, smooth and slightly pointed. Its blossoms are white-pink and have markedly long purple anthers. Caper bushes often grow wild and tend not to be too picky about soil quality and water. Today, caper bushes are grown on large plantations, mainly in Turkey, Morocco, Spain and on Majorca. Unripe, still closed buds are harvested. Let the buds wither slightly and put them in oil, salty water, vinegar or into a mixture made of vinegar and salt.

RELATED SPECIES: During hard times, the buds of marsh marigold (Caltha palustris) or Indian cress (Tropaeolum majus) were used as substitutes for capers. Despite the fact that they are not botanically related, they contain similar substances which imitate the taste of genuine capers.

MEDICINAL USE: The ancient Greeks knew the positive effects of capers on improving appetite, promoting digestion and strengthening the stomach. Capers can alleviate coughing or be used externally for eye infections. Spleen diseases are healed with capers as well.

CORNICHON DE CAPRES

Caper fruits, caper berries or caper apples ("*cornichon de capres*," or 'caper cucumbers') are canned in the same manner and are rarely available. Their taste is very intense. They can be distinguished from capers because the fruit is attached to the herbaceous stem. Ideal with antipasti!

CAPERS ARE DIVIDED INTO QUALITY CLASSES: Gruesas (more than 13 mm), Fines (11–13 mm), Capottes (9–11 mm), Capucines (8–9 mm), Surfines (7–8 mm), and Nonpareilles (the smallest capers are the most precious and their diameter is less than 7 mm).

HAVE YOU EVER TASTED IT?

TARTAR SAUCE AND CAPERS
Make 2 hard-boiled eggs, remove the shells and dice very finely. Put 1 cup mayonnaise in a dish. Wash 4 anchovy fillets in cold water and dry. Cut finely together with 4 tablespoons capers. Mix the eggs with about 8 tablespoons of minced herbs (e. g. Italian parsley, chives, tarragon, chervil, and dill) and the mayonnaise. Season the tartar sauce with salt, pepper, sugar, a little lemon juice and a few dashes of Worcestershire sauce.

IN THE KITCHEN

AROMA:
The smell of capers is slightly spicy and slightly sour. Combined with brine, the taste becomes slightly acrid and piquant.

USE:
Capers are used in sauces and remoulades as well as in tartar sauce and salads. One puts this spice into veal dishes, such as the popular Vitello tonnato, in Italian cuisine.

BUYING/STORING:
Capers are available in every well-supplied supermarket. They can be stored in airtight jars in brine for at least 1 year. Their quality and price correspond to their size: smaller capers are finer and pricier.

TIPS FOR COOKING:
To preserve an open jar of capers, add a little olive oil before closing the jar. The oil will prevent the capers from becoming moldy and extends their durability.
Add capers to a dish only at the very end of cooking because they lose their flavor if cooked longer.

Capsicum
Chili

Origin:

America

Edible part:

Use:

Property:
!

FAMILY: Potato (*Solanaceae*)

SYNONYMS: -

FORMS OF USE: Fruit, fresh and dried as well as crushed and ground

ORIGIN: All chili spices and peppers originated from the so-called bird pepper, chili tepin. Although native to Central and South America, chili plants are now cultivated almost everywhere.

REMARKS: Depending on the particular form, chili fruits are round or pointed, green, yellow or red. They are green when unripe and eventually turn red. However, the green fruits can be used for eating and seasoning as well. Furthermore, they all contain much capsaicin, vitamin C and vitamin A.

RELATED SPECIES: The "foremother" is Capsicum tepin. All chili siliquas, spice pepper and vegetable peppers originate from it.

MEDICINAL USE: The Indians used chili as a medicine. Chili promotes blood circulation, has antibacterial properties and, if consumed in high doses, induces perspiration.

DID YOU KNOW …?
There are hundreds of varieties of chili. They can be divided into five species:
Capsicum annum: Most common types of chili, such as vegetable pepper and spice pepper, pepperoni and pepe-

rocnini, belong to this kind. Only one bloom hangs from the branch of a plant up to 5 feet high. Most types like jalapeno chili, New Mexican and Ornamental Piquin, belong to *Capsicum annuum.*

Capsicum frutescens: 1 - 2 or (rarely) up to 4 upright blooms can grow from a branch. The fruits grow upright later. Very hot, wild types like Tabasco belong to this group.

Capsicum pubescens: It is the only conditionally frost-resistant form (up to 23°F). It has distinctive leaves, violet blooms and mostly black seeds. The most common types are Rocoto and Manzano.

Capsicum chinense: This variant with big leaves has 2-5 blooms on each branch. Habanero and Scotch Bonnet are the best-known representatives of this group. The reinforcement of calyxes is typical.

Capsicum baccatum: This species has big leaves and one bloom per branch. It is resistant to cold up to 32°F and comprises only hot varieties. Red Sevina, a Habanero special culture, is the hottest of all.

IN THE KITCHEN

AROMA:
Depending on its particular form, chili is hot or distinctively sharp.

USE:
Chili and chili powder are popular spices in Asian cuisine, and Thai dishes in particular. They add pungent spiciness to dishes from Latin America, Mexico, and the Caribbean as well as southern European countries.

BUYING/STORING:
Chili is available fresh or pickled in jars in well-supplied supermarkets. If you keep fresh chili in the vegetable compartment of your refrigerator, it will last for several weeks. Dried siliquas remain aromatic for years if stored in a dry and dark place.

TIPS FOR COOKING:
Dried chili is hotter than fresh siliquas. The smaller the size, the sharper the taste. Its inconspicuous seeds are responsible for the sharpness. If you prefer it milder, remove the seeds and partition walls.

IMPORTANT WARNING:

Do not eat chili if you have open wounds in the areas of the pharynx, gullet or gastrointestinal tract. Even the smallest wounds burn painfully when in contact with chili. It is best to wear gloves when cleaning and cutting chilies or to wash hands properly after cooking.

Capsicum annuum
Paprika

Origin:

America

Edible part:

Use:

FAMILY: Potato (*Solanaceae*)

SYNONYMS: -

FORMS OF USE: Fruit with seeds, dried or ground.

ORIGIN: Columbus brought the paprika plant back from his first voyage to America. It is cultivated mainly in the Balkans, Hungary, in the Basque areas of Spain and France as well as in South and Central America.

REMARKS: Paprika is an annual which grows up to 24 inches high. It has wide, deep green leaves and yellowish-green blooms. Narrow, 4 inch long, deep red siliquas are pointed. There are more than 30 types of paprika, mild and spicy, wild and cultivated. They differ considerably from one another. Be careful not to confuse them.

RELATED SPECIES: Paprika is closely related to vegetable pepper and chili siliqua is a close relative as well.

MYTHOLOGY: "Sweet like a sin and hot as a devil" is what they say about the taste of paprika. Its reputation as a spice

with healing properties caused it to spread like wild fire in the Old World, conquering Spain, the Balkans, North Africa as well as India.

MEDICINAL USE: Paprika is rich in vitamin C and carotinoides. It promotes appetite, strengthens blood circulation, protects blood vessels and has anti-thrombus properties. It supports the secretion of digestive juices and has antiseptic as well as perspiratory effects in high doses.

DID YOU KNOW ...?
Harvested paprika siliquas are dried and ground. Ripe siliquas have little flesh and juice, but contain seeds on partition walls inside. The walls and seeds are particularly rich in capsaicin. The more walls and seeds you grind, the hotter the paprika powder. You can distinguish five degrees of taste, quality and hotness in paprika:

Select paprika: It contains the best fruits, is mildly aromatic and gives an appetizing red color to dishes. This type is the proper choice for people who do not like to make their food too hot. It is used industrially to color tomato purée and tomato ketchup.

Sweet paprika: is the most common type. It is very spicy and mildly hot and colors dishes dark red.

Semi-sweet paprika: It has much more spicing power and, therefore, goes well with nutritious meat dishes like mutton roast and Hungarian goulash.

Red paprika: It is the hottest paprika you can buy and is mostly used in Hungarian and Viennese cuisines. It colors dishes deep red.

Hot pepper: Its taste is extremely sharp. It is produced of fruits, seeds and partition walls and is not available in some counties.

In the kitchen

Aroma:
Depending on the quality, it is mildly aromatic up to very hot.

Use:
You can see that paprika is the Hungarian national spice: paprika steak, szegedine style goulash, Serbian rice meat, and paprika chicken are classic dishes which could not have become famous without paprika. It goes well with beef, pork, lamb and poultry. Many fish, soups, egg and cheese dishes and salads require paprika.

Buying/storing:
Paprika is available in every grocery. Four different degrees of quality are available. Store it in an airproof container in a cool, dark place. It loses its aroma in about 1 year, becoming brown and stale.

Tips for cooking:
Never add paprika to hot fat or the sugar contained in paprika caramelizes. Season dishes only at the end of cooking. The sweeter and milder the paprika, the sooner you can add higher amounts of it to the pot.

Capsicum frutescens
Cayenne pepper

FAMILY: Potato (*Solanaceae*)

SYNONYMS: Bird pepper, tabasco, chile pepper, goat pepper, spur pepper

FORMS OF USE: Fruits with seeds, dried and ground.

ORIGIN: Cayenne peppers are the fruits of Capsicum frutescens. The plant is native to South and Central America and is cultivated in all tropical regions in the world today.

REMARKS: The plant of Capsicum frutescens bears 1 inch long, thin, pointed and cylindrical orange or red fruits. Its berries are dried after being harvested and ground finely. Cayenne pepper, in contrast to paprika, has a significantly higher amount of capsaicin, which causes its sharpness.

RELATED SPECIES: Cayenne pepper is very closely related to paprika. Chili is also a close relative.

MEDICINAL USE: Cayenne pepper is rich in vitamin C and vitamin A. It promotes blood circulation and prevents cold.

DID YOU KNOW ...?
Cayenne pepper is probably named after the Cayenne port in Guyana, a seaport on Devils Island and a notorious place of exile. However, this town was never an important export port, of Cayenne pepper in particular.

HAVE YOU EVER TASTED IT?

CREOLE SHRIMP STEW
Peel 1 lb shrimp, remove the meat, wash in cold water and dry. Cut two similar-sized fillets of 1 lb chicken breast fillet. Peel 2 onions and 2 garlic cloves and mince. Wash 1 green pepper, cut it in halves, remove the stem, white partition walls and seeds and cut the flesh into small dice. Wash 4 celery ribs and dice. Cut 1 can of tomatoes into little pieces and set aside along with the tomato juice. Heat about 4 tablespoons of vegetable oil, roast the shrimp on both sides and season with salt and Cayenne pepper. Take out and put aside.

Sautée the chicken in the hot oil, and season with a little Cayenne pepper, salt and cumin powder. Roast the chicken, add onion and garlic and stew.

Take out the remaining vegetable and season everything with salt, pepper and thyme. Add the canned tomatoes and tomato juice and simmer the stew in an open pot for about 10 minutes. Heat 1 quart of chicken broth and add to the stew together with about 1 cup of rice. Simmer everything for about 20 minutes. When the rice is boiled, heat the shrimp in the stew. Season once again and serve hot.

IN THE KITCHEN

AROMA:
Cayenne pepper is about twenty times hotter than paprika, but not as spicy.

USE:
Cayenne pepper is commonly used in South American and Creole cuisines. However, it is an important ingredient in many Indian and Asian dishes as well. Cayenne pepper seasons nutritious stews and soups. It goes well with fish and seafood, eggs and rice dishes.

IMPORTANT WARNING:

Do not eat Cayenne pepper if you have open wounds in the pharynx, gullet or gastrointestinal tract. It is extremely hot and can result in unbearable pain.

BUYING/STORING:
Cayenne pepper is available in well-supplied groceries. It should be stored in an airproof container in a cool, dark place. It keeps its aroma for about three months.

TIPS FOR COOKING:
Use Cayenne pepper in small amounts or it will dominate the dish unpleasantly.

If you put too much Cayenne pepper in a dish by accident, it is possible to fix it by adding a raw grated potato or some breadcrumbs to the dish. The burning of Cayenne pepper in your throat cannot be soothed with water. On the contrary, the sharpness is even heightened in the pharynx. It is better to drink a yogurt shake.

Carum carvi
Caraway

Origin:

Europe

Edible part:

Use:

✗ 𝔄

FAMILY: Carrot (*Apiaceae*)

SYNONYMS: Carvi, alcaravia, kummel

FORMS OF USE: Seeds, dried, whole or ground

ORIGIN: Caraway is one of the oldest European spices. Dishes were seasoned with caraway already in Neolithic times. It grows wild in Europe, North Africa, western Asia and India. Today it is cultivated mainly in the Netherlands, Poland and Hungary.

REMARKS: Caraway is a biennial plant. It resembles beet plants in the first year, grows to 3 feet in height during the second year and blooms in white umbels. The blooms change into seeds, which are eventually cut, thrashed and dried. Caraway contains many essential oils, carvon and limonene, which are responsible for its distinctive taste.

RELATED SPECIES: Caraway is closely related to cumin. Caraway is considered a northern spice and cumin is a spice of the south. Generally speaking, the distinction

holds true. However, caraway is often used in Indian cuisine as well.

MYTHOLOGY: People in the Middle Ages believed that caraway seed could chase away ghosts and demons.

MEDICINAL USE: Caraway is an old spice. It promotes digestion and is used to cure flatulence. Mix 2 teaspoons caraway with 1 cup of water. Steep caraway in hot water in a covered cup for about 5 minutes and strain. Drink 2 -

3 cups after eating every day. Drinking tea prepared from equal parts of caraway, fennel, anis and dried nettle can stimulate lactation.

DID YOU KNOW ...?
People in northern Germany have a liquor called "kummel" distilled from grain and only the essential oil contained in the caraway seeds is added to it.

IN THE KITCHEN

AROMA:
Caraway is spicy, aromatic and slightly hot like lemon.

USE:
Caraway is best alone and can rarely be combined with other spices. It is used to season cabbage dishes like sauerkraut, Savoy cabbage and cabbage potages as well as cabbage rolls. It goes well with nutritious, stewed dishes like lamb, pork, goose and baked potatoes. Piquant breads, such as gingerbread, are also seasoned with caraway.

BUYING/STORING:
Seeds are available in almost every grocery whole or ground. Keep them in a closed container in a dry, dark place. Caraway loses its aroma very gradually and will keep for a long time if stored properly.

TIPS FOR COOKING:
Young caraway leaves can also be eaten. They go well with nutritious salads and their appearance, but not taste, is slightly reminiscent of parsley. Whole caraway seeds should be crushed in a mortar to fully develop their aroma.

Cinnamomum aromaticum
Cassia

Origin:

Asia

Edible part:

Use:

FAMILY: Laurel (*Lauraceae*)

SYNONYMS: Chinese cassia

FORMS OF USE: Dried bark, divided in pieces or ground

ORIGIN: Cassia is native to southern China. It is cultivated in Indonesia, Vietnam and Japan as well.

REMARKS: Cassia trees are grown on plantations and their bark is processed similarly to the bark of the cinnamon tree. When dried, the bark of the cassia tree is darker and much thicker than cinnamon. It is usually available in ground form and is difficult to distinguish from cinnamon.

MEDICINAL USE: Cassia is of great importance in Chinese medicine, where it is used to promote appetite and digestion. The spice is known for its antibacterial and anti-fungicide properties.

In the kitchen

AROMA:
Cassia is highly aromatic and slightly bitter in taste.
It should be used slightly more carefully than
Ceylon cinnamon.

USE:
Cassia can be used similarly to cinnamon in cooking. It goes well with bitter, fruity rhubarb, plums
and apples. However, you can season meat and
game dishes with it as well.

BUYING/STORING:
Cassia, both in powder and stick forms, should be stored
in an airproof container in a dark, dry place. It is often sold
instead of cinnamon in stores. Sticks, however, are available only in spice stores.

TIPS FOR COOKING:
Cassia is an ingredient in Chinese five-spice mixes and is
used instead of cinnamon in classic Asian cuisine. Cassia
powder should be used sparingly because it may over-
power dishes with its bitter taste. It should not come into
contact with very hot oil because it burns quickly.

Cinnamomum verum
Cinnamon

FAMILY: Laurel (*Lauraceae*)

SYNONYMS: -

FORMS OF USE: Dried bark, divided into pieces or ground

ORIGIN: Cinnamon is native to Ceylon, today known as Sri Lanka. It is cultivated in Indonesia, Madagascar, the Lesser Antilles and Central America as well.

REMARKS: Cinnamon trees are grown in plantations. In nature, cinnamon trees grow up to 66 feet high. If cultivated, they are kept smaller in order to make the annual trimming of 6 feet long sprouts easier. Cinnamon sticks are made by stripping off the bark of the trees and making bundles of it. The bundles of bark are then covered and fermented for 1 –2 days. Afterwards, the external and internal layers of bark are removed and the rest of the clean bark is dried in the sun. The bark curls during this process. The pieces are rolled together to form a stick of cinnamon. The best-quality cinnamon has a light color and feels like rolled, dried paper. The thinner the piece of bark, the finer the taste.

RELATED SPECIES: There are about 275 different types of cinnamon trees. At least five of them are used to produce cinnamon spice. Besides the Ceylon cinnamon tree, the Padang cinnamon tree (*Cinnamomum burmanii*) and the cassia cinnamon tree (*Cinnamomum aromaticum*) act as as substitute spices.

MYTHOLOGY: In *The Arabian Nights*, Scheherazade recounts the fantastical legend of the origin of cinnamon. Cinnamon, she says, grows on the floor of a secret lake.

According to another fairy tale, cinnamon is brought by cinnamon birds who collect the spice in their nests. In order to procure the precious cinnamon sticks, they must be shot down from their nests in high trees with bows and arrows.

MEDICINAL USE: Hippocrates emphasized the importance of cinnamon in medicine in about 500 BC. Cinnamon bark oil is highly antiseptic. It promotes blood circulation in the body and is good for the heart.

DID YOU KNOW ...?
The quality is determined by the color and delicacy of the bark that is expressed in "Ekelle." The best cinnamon can be extremely expensive. Industrially, cinnamon is used in perfumery and soap production. It is an important ingredient in liquors as well as in medicines promoting digestion.

IN THE KITCHEN

AROMA:
Cinnamon is highly aromatic, fine and sweet. However, its taste is sometimes bitter.

USE:
There are many ways to use cinnamon. It is used in sweet dishes, cakes, chocolate drinks, fruit juice, mulled wine, tea and honey, and is added to rice milk in some countries. In Asian cuisine, it is common to use cinnamon to season meat and fish dishes as well as pilafs and curry. Cola drinks, lemonades and chewing gums often contain cinnamon oil.

IMPORTANT WARNING:

Cinnamon oil, prepared from bark, can irritate skin. Therefore, mild oil prepared from cinnamon leaves is suitable for baths and massages because of its relaxing and antispasmodic properties. It is a good way to treat gastrointestinal disorders or strained muscles.

BUYING/STORING:
Cinnamon powder, ground from crushed sticks, is more precious than sticks. Both cinnamon sticks and powder should be stored in airproof containers in a dark, dry place.

TIPS FOR COOKING:
Cinnamon is the most important ingredient in gingerbread, which contains coriander, anis, Chinese anise, cloves, orange and lemon peel, cardamom, nutmeg, mace and pimento. Mulled wine spices include cinnamon sticks, Chinese anise, cloves and cardamom.

Citrus hystrix
Kaffir lime

FAMILY: Rue (*Rutaceae*)

SYNONYMS: Leech lime, djerek purut, Ichang lime, Makrut, Djeruk purut

FORMS OF USE: Leaves, fresh and dried, fruits, peel in particular

ORIGIN: Kaffir lime tree is native to Southeast Asia and is especially widespread in Thailand and Indonesia.

REMARKS: The kaffir lime tree is little, only up to 9 feet high. The leaves have a very peculiar petiole with a wing as large as the leaf blade itself. Their surface is glossy dark green and light green underneath. Round citrus fruits develop from little white blossoms. Their peel can be used to season as well.

IN THE KITCHEN

AROMA:
The smell of Kaffir lime leaves as well as the peel of its fruit is strongly reminiscent of lemons.

USE:
Kaffir lime leaves are an important spice in Thai as well as Indonesian cuisine. They are used to spice soups, dips and curry, fish, and poultry dishes.

BUYING/STORING:
Both fresh and dried kaffir lime leaves are available in Asian stores. Fresh leaves can be stored in a bag in a refrigerator for a few weeks. Dried leaves should be stored in an airproof container in a cool, dark place. They lose their aroma after about one year. Therefore, do not buy the leaves in large quantities.

TIPS FOR COOKING:
Kaffir lime leaves go well with coconut milk, ginger, galangal, garlic and chili.
Whole kaffir lime leaves are cooked and removed from the dish before being served. Sometimes they are minced and placed in a dish.
When you want to stock up on kaffir lime leaves, freeze fresh leaves. They maintain their aroma best this way.

Coriandrum sativum
Coriander

FAMILY: Carrot (*Apiaceae*)

SYNONYMS: Chinese parsley, cilantro

FORMS OF USE: Seeds, dried, whole or ground, and leaves, fresh, root

ORIGIN: An herb native to and common in southern Europe and western Asia for thousands of years. Today, coriander is spread throughout the Mediterranean, the Netherlands, the Balkans, Russia, India and America.

PROPERTIES: The 12 – 24 inch high plant is not picky about the quality of its soil. Its leaves are fan-shaped in the lower part and pinnate in the upper part. The blossoms form an umbel, bloom white and develop into globular, round, yellow-brown ribbed fruits. Their diameter is 1.5 – 3 mm. The seeds are dried and ground after harvesting.

RELATED SPECIES: Coriander resembles parsley in many ways. Both their leaves and their blossoms are very similar and can be easily confused. Both herbs are used in

a similar manner in cooking because their leaves tolerate neither heat nor drying. You can make broth from its roots.

MYTHOLOGY: Coriander is one of the oldest cultivated plants. It was mentioned in the Bible as one of the bitter herbs of the Passover feast. Seeds were discovered in archaeological finds among cultural relics from the Neolithic Era. Traces of coriander found in the tombs of the Pharaohs show that coriander was also appreciated in ancient Egypt.

MEDICINAL USE: coriander contains essential oils which help stomach and intestinal disorders and have a sedative effect on nerves. Coriander is flatulent because it stimulates the activity of intestinal musculature, causing intestinal convulsions and strengthening the stomach.

GARAM MASALA

The Indian word "*masala*" means a "spice mix." Garam masalab, however, is not one particular combination of spices. Depending on geographical regions and personal tastes, each Indian cook mixes their own garam masala according to an individual recipe. Generally, you can distinguish between garam masala powder and paste, although they both contain coriander, cumin, cloves, nutmeg and pepper. The pastes are mixed with chili peppers and often mint and green coriander.

TIPS FOR COOKING:

The aroma of coriander intensifies when the seeds are crushed in a mortar or roasted in a pan without any fat.

Coriander goes well with cumin, chili, fresh mint and garlic.

IN THE KITCHEN

AROMA:
The aroma of the fruit is pleasantly nutty and spicy. The smell and taste of coriander haulm as well as its roots is very strong and sometimes you must get used to it!

USE:
Coriander seeds are classic spices added to baked goods or used as a spice for dishes containing cabbage, potatoes and legumes. They enhance the taste of roast fish, poultry and meat dishes and complement chutney, plum jam and pickled vegetables as well. The herb is mainly used as a spice in Thai, Indian, Mexican and Brazilian cuisines. Coriander seeds are added to liquors and vermouth and were used in beer production during the Middle Ages as well.

BUYING/STORING:
Coriander seeds, whole or ground, are available in the spice section of well-supplied supermarkets. Green coriander is available in the vegetable section throughout the year. Coriander seeds should be stored in an air-proof closed container in a cool, dark place to keep their aroma for up to 1 year. Ground coriander loses its taste very fast. The leaves and roots of coriander can only be used fresh because they lose their flavor if dried.

Crocus sativus
Saffron

Origin:

Asia

Edible part:

Use:

Property:
!

FAMILY: Iris (*Iridaceae*)

SYNONYMS: Saffron crocus, azafran

FORMS OF USE: Blossoms, dried, whole or ground

ORIGIN: Saffron is native to western Asia and is cultivated in India, China, Iran and Iraq as well as throughout the Mediterranean region, particularly Spain. The best saffron is supposedly from the "La Mancha" plateau.

PROPERTIES: Saffron is a type of crocus. Its blossoms are lilac and bloom from September to October. Its leaves are long, narrow and similar to grass. The saffron petals of the blossoms are nipped off manually during their six-week blooming time. They must be dried as quickly as possible and they lose about 80 percent of their original weight during the process. About 200,000 to 400,000 petals are needed for 1 pound of saffron spice. Saffron is, therefore, available only in small quantities at a relatively high price even today. A dish flavored with saffron is definately a special treat.

RELATED SPECIES: Saffron is related to the crocus.

MYTHOLOGY: It is said that the ancient Phoenicians baked cakes spiced with saffron in honor of the goddess of love when they wanted to be lucky in love. The Roman Marcus Aurelius allegedly bathed in saffron water because it tinted his skin and increased his virility, or so he believed!

MEDICINAL USE: Doctor Dioscorides from Asia Minor described the therapeutic effects of saffron in his work "De materia medica," published in about 60–78 AD. It was thought to be a diuretic, helpful for calming inflammations

and was mixed with water and used for "eye and ear effusions." Heart-strengthening and aphrodisiac effects of saffron were known before Christ and it was used as a hallucinogen and opium substitute as well in Asia Minor, Egypt, Greece and Italy.

DID YOU KNOW ...?
Saffron is the most expensive spice in the world today, prompting the innovation of cheaper substitutes and supplements to saffron powder such as safflower, safflower seeds, thistle oil or turmeric. Cutting saffron was punished with death by burning in Nuremberg during the Middle Ages. Seasoning with safflower is common in the Arab world today and many tourists buy it in bazaars as a cheaper version of saffron.

Highly prized saffron fibers are dark red and they feel elastic or flabby. Their typical yellow color changes only when diluted in water.

IN THE KITCHEN

AROMA:

Saffron tastes acrid, bitter or piquant and tints food yellow.

USE:

Saffron is used to color cakes and sweet baked goods. However, saffron is crucial in many classic piquant dishes such as Spanish paella, French bouillabaisse and Italian risotto alla milanese. It is added to many Arab rice dishes and goes well with lamb, poultry and fish. Saffron seasons very nicely and colors food attractively.

BUYING/STORING:

Saffron is available in fibers or ground. The fibers are preferable because they remain aromatic longer. Besides, you can be sure that you bought genuine saffron if you buy it in the fiber form. It should be stored in an air-proof container in a dark, dry place.

TIPS FOR COOKING:

You obtain the finest aroma when you crush the saffron fibers with a mortar. Saffron powder can be added directly to dishes.

IMPORTANT WARNING:

Saffron consumed during pregnancy can cause miscarriage. It has narcotizing effect if consumed in larger quantities and even a small dosage of 2 – 2½ teaspoons can be fatal.

Cuminum cyminum
Cumin

Origin:

Asia

Edible part:

Use:

FAMILY: Carrot (*Apiaceae*)

SYNONYMS: Comino

FORMS OF USE: Seeds, dried, whole and ground

ORIGIN: Cumin is native to the eastern Mediterranean region and Egypt. Today, it is principally cultivated in North African and Middle Eastern countries, India and Mexico.

PROPERTIES: This creeping plant grows only 12 inches high and has dark green leaves and white - almost lilac - blossoms, which develop into fruits. Cumin is visually very similar to caraway. However, black cumin is dark coffee brown and is a spice as well as an herb.

RELATED SPECIES: Besides common brown cumin, there is black cumin as well. It is called Cashmere cumin and is used mainly in Iran, Pakistan and in northern India, where it grows wild. Its seeds are black and smaller than those of regular cumin.

MYTHOLOGY: The Egyptians put cumin in the pyramids where they buried their pharaohs. Cumin was probably regarded as a medicine at the time. The Romans used it instead of pepper and ground it into a paste to use as a spread on bread. It was grown in cloister gardens under the reign of Charlemagne. In modern times, cumin oil is used in heavy, oriental perfumes.

MEDICINAL USE: Eating cumin has very positive effects on digestion. It releases convulsions and brings relief in the abdominal area in cases of colic, diarrhea and dysmenorrhea. When used in greater quantities, it helps to cure the diseases of upper airways. Or chew a few cumin seeds for about 2 minutes and spit them out! It stimulates the appetite, cleans blood and has a sedative effect.

It was used to treat pulmonary diseases in ancient Egypt.

DID YOU KNOW ...?

Pliny, a Roman scholar, mentions in his works that a rich Roman, C. Julyus Vinder, won the post of Propretor in Galicia through deception. He was drinking an extract of cumin and went to the emperor Nero, promising him to appoint him heir of his property if the emperor complied with his request amd granted him the post. Thanks to the cumin, the greedy emperor was disappointed.

TIPS FOR COOKING:

Cumin is a suitable spice for mixtures because it goes well with other exotic spices. Cumin should be used reasonably because it has very strong taste. To intensify the taste of cumin, roast it in a hot pan without fat.

IN THE KITCHEN

AROMA:
Cumin taste is pleasant, fresh and sharply aromatic. Its taste resembles that of caraway very remotely.

USE:
Cumin is used particularly in Arab, Far Eastern and Latin American cuisines. It belongs among the spices used in Indonesian rice dishes and is added to many types of Indian chutney, mango chutney, for example. It is also used in Arab and Mexican meat dishes like chili con carne and it can be present in bread and cheese as well as in bitter and herbal liquors.

Cumin is essential in spice mixes like garam masala, tandoori and curry.

BUYING/STORING:
Cumin is available in spice stores either whole or ground. If whole seeds are kept in an air-proof closed container in a cool, dry and dark place, they will last more than 1 year. In powder form, cumin loses its aroma and taste quickly.

Curcuma longa
Turmeric

Origin:

Asia

Edible part:

Use:

FAMILY: Ginger (*Zingiberaceae*)

SYNONYMS: Curcuma domestica, curcuma

FORMS OF USE: Root, fresh and dried, whole or ground

Origin: The plant has been cultivated for more than 2,000 years in Southeast and southern Asia. While 80 percent of worldwide production is in India today, tumeric continues to be cultivated in Indonesia. It is also grown in South America.

PROPERTIES: The turmeric plant can grow 3 – 8 feet high and its lanceolate leaves are very big and wide. Its blossom is yellow and similar to the flowers of lilies. Its tuberous rhizome resembles ginger. The turmeric tuber is rounder and narrower, the bark is yellow and brown and the flesh is orange. The root is boiled after being harvested and dried. Then the external layer is removed. Dried turmeric roots, which look like small branches, are ground to make curry powder.

RELATED SPECIES: Turmeric is related to ginger and galangal.

MYTHOLOGY: In the Vedic culture of India, turmeric is a holy and important spice. The cowls of Buddhist monks were dyed with turmeric until recently. In Christian culttures, tumeric is also used as a natural dye for Easter eggs.

MEDICINAL USE: The yellow color called curcumin promotes the emptying of the gall bladder. The essential oil stimulates bile production in the liver. You can successfully use turmeric for stomach and intestinal diseases caused by a reduced excretion of bile.

HAVE YOU EVER TASTED IT?

MANGO CHUTNEY
Pit, peel and chop 1 mango. Peel a 1 inch piece of ginger, 3 garlic cloves and 1 onion and chop finely. Wash and chop 1 red chili pepper. Sauté the ginger, garlic and onion. Add 1 tablespoon turmeric ½ and ⅛ teaspoon garam masala, mango, chili and ½ cup brown sugar. Add 5 tablespoons white wine vinegar and 5 tablespoons white wine and mix until the sugar is diluted. Then simmer uncovered for about 15 minutes, stirring from time to time. Add about 3 tablespoons of raisins during the last 5 minutes of cooking. When the consistency of the chutney thickens, pour into a small jar.

IN THE KITCHEN

AROMA:
Turmeric smells like ginger and tastes piquant, but its aroma is stronger than ginger.

USE:
Turmeric is the most important ingredient in curry powder. It is used mainly in Indian dishes, but can be found in East African cuisine as well. It is used to season rice and pasta dishes, soups, sauces and mayonnaise. It goes well with fish and seafood as well as with poultry, eggs, vegetable curry and chutney.

BUYING/STORING:
Buy ground turmeric only in small quantities because it loses its aroma fast. Keep in an air-proof closed container in a dry, dark place. Treat dried roots in the same manner. And when you manage to buy fresh turmeric, store it, like ginger, in the vegetable compartment of the refridgerator for several weeks.

TIPS FOR COOKING:
Turmeric can be used as a cheaper substitute for saffron. Worcestershire sauce and mustard contain turmeric as well.

Cymbopogon citratus
Lemongrass

Origin:

Asia

Edible part:
🌿

Use:
✗

FAMILY: Grass (*Poaceae*)

SYNONYMS: West Indian lemongrass

FORMS OF USE: Stalks, fresh and dried, cut into pieces and ground

ORIGIN: Lemon grass is native to tropical Southeast Asia. The plant is cultivated in India, Africa, Australia and America today.

PROPERTIES: Up to 6 feet high tropical grass grows from a tuberous root. It is a perennial and grows in thick tufts. The long, pointed leaves of the herb are similar to grass. Only very young, thin leaves, finely cut, can be used for cooking. Older leaves are tasteless and tough.

IN THE KITCHEN

AROMA:
Lemon grass is very sour, fresh and similar to lemon with a trace of rose odor.

USE:
Lemon grass is used mainly in Thai, Vietnamese, Indonesian and Indian cuisines. It is used to season soups, stewed fish and poultry dishes. It goes well with coconut, chili and green coriander.

BUYING/STORING:
Dried lemon grass is available in Asian specialty stores and groceries carrying natural food. Fresh lemon grass is available in Asian markets.

TIPS FOR COOKING:
Use a saw knife to cut fresh lemon grass because the plant is very tough.

Lemon grass is cooked in fondue, but is not eaten raw because it is fibrous and too tough to chew.

However, you can prepare a refreshing tea using lemon grass. Let it steep for at least 10 minutes because the aroma is released very slowly.

Elettaria cardamomum
Cardamom

Origin:

Asia

Edible part:

Use:

FAMILY: Ginger (*Zingiberaceae*)

SYNONYMS: Lesser cardamom, Ceylon cardamom

FORMS OF USE: Seeds, dried, whole or ground

ORIGIN: Cardamom is native to South India, Ceylon and Malaysia. It is cultivated in India and Guatemala as well.

PROPERTIES: Cardamom is a reedy, perennial plant which can grow up to 5 feet (1.5 m). Its blossoms are light yellow and grow into small, green fruit pods. The fruits can be harvested during the third year. Therefore, one has to keep watching the plant because the seeds ripen throughout the year. You must harvest the seed pods before they ripen, or "jump out," and dry them in a drying chamber in the sun. The seeds are the spice and contain fine aromatic essential oils. They are left in the pods in order to protect their aroma and they are available ground as a reddish-gray powder.
Since the spice is expensive, its light seed cases are often ground and added to the spice. You can distinguish

between pure cardamom seed and "cardamom with ground seedcases," according to color.

RELATED SPECIES: Its close relatives include brown Ceylon cardamom (Elletaria major), which tastes bitter and is often used as a cardamom substitute, and paradise pepper (Aframomum melegueta). Their taste is sharp and peppery, similar to the taste of cardamom.

MYTHOLOGY: Some people believe that cardamom increases male sexual appetite and stamina, an effect attributed to the spice's iodine content.

MEDICINAL USE: The best known effect of cardamom is that it promotes digestion. It helps cure flatulence and eases stomachaches and cramps as well. Chewing the seeds refreshes the breath and improves the voice. Cardamom even contains detoxifying enzymes which relieve hangovers. It is regarded by many as an aphrodisiac.

HAVE YOU EVER TASTED IT?

CARDAMOM TEA
Crush slightly 12 green cardamom pods in a mortar. Steep in about 6 cups of hot water for 10 minutes with a long, wide strip of untreated orange peel. Add 2 – 3 tablespoons of Ceylon tea and infuse for another 3 to 5 minutes. Strain the tea and serve with sugar and milk.

CARDAMOM ICE TEA
Mix cold cardamom tea and fresh pressed orange or lime juice. Put crushed ice in one third of a glass with 2 tablespoons brown sugar and add the cardamom tea and fruit juice.

IN THE KITCHEN

AROMA:
The aroma of cardamom is very fine, sweet and sharp. Its aftertaste resembles a mix of lemon, camphor and bergamot.

USE:
Cardamom is added to mulled wine and gingerbread. It is a significant part of curry mixes. If well dosed, it goes well with cakes, baked goods, meat dishes, pickles and herrings, sausages, pâtés and liquors as well as with whisky. Coffee and tea in Asian countries is enhanced with cardamom. Cardamom pods strengthen the aroma of Bedouin coffee.

BUYING/STORING:
Whole cardamom seeds or pods are available in spice stores. Ground cardamom is available in well-supplied supermarkets as well. The best way to store cardamom is to put it in a bowl and keep it in a cool, dry and dark place. Ground seeds lose their aroma very fast.

TIPS FOR COOKING:
Cardamom develops its aroma best when roasted in a pan without any fat. It should be added at the begining of cooking because it develops its full taste only when heated.

Ferula asafoetida
Devil's dung

Origin:

Asia

Edible part:

Use:

FAMILY: Carrot (*Apiaceae*)

SYNONYMS: Ferula, food of the gods, asafetida, asafetida gum, asant

FORMS OF USE: Juice of roots, resin or ground

ORIGIN: Devil's dung is native to eastern Iran and Afghanistan, where it flourishes in salt steppes.

PROPERTIES: Devil's dung forms only one rosette at first. During the fifth year, 3 – 9 feet long and 4 inch thick herbaceous stems develop. Leaves are pinnate; yellow-green blossoms are many-rayed umbels. Juice seeps out of the roots when cut. It solidifies in air and it is almost as hard as caoutchouc resin. Since the resin cannot be ground alone, fenugreek seeds are mixed into the powder.

MEDICINAL USE: Devil's dung has a calming effect, stimulates the nervous system and the distribution of sex hormones, relieves spasms, and cures stomach, liver and gall bladder maladies.

IN THE KITCHEN

AROMA:
The taste of devil's dung resembles the taste of garlic, but it is rather sharp and slightly bitter.

USE:
Devil's dung was a popular spice in Europe at the time of the Romans and during the Middle Ages. It is still used in India, Pakistan, Iran and Iraq to spice stewed meat and vegetable dishes.

BUYING/STORING:
Devil's dung as caoutchouc resin is rarely available even in Asian specialty stores. Ground devil's dung is preferable to resin because it is easier to measure. You can buy it in natural food stores or in spice shops. It should be kept in an air-proof closed container in a dark, dry place.

TIPS FOR COOKING:
Devil's dung loses its penetrating garlic taste and smell during cooking.
Measure the spice carefully. Always dilute the resin in hot water.
If you need Devil's dung to prepare a dish and none is available, you can substitute garlic and onion.

Foeniculum vulgare
Fennel

FAMILY: Carrot (*Apiaceae*)

SYNONYMS: Common fennel

FORMS OF USE: Seeds, whole or ground

ORIGIN: Fennel is native to the Mediterranean region, but it is cultivated in India, China and Japan, the Balkans, Denmark, Germany, Great Britain and the United States.

PROPERTIES: Fennel grows up to 5 feet high and has pinnate, blue-green leaves similar to dill. It has yellow blossoms from July to September. The small blossoms grow in umbels 3 – 12 mm long and 2 – 4 mm wide. Fennel seeds are harvested mechanically, thrashed and dried. Compared to other spices, its fruits are green even when dried. The more intense the green color, the better the quality.

RELATED SPECIES: Spice fennel is related to vegetable fennel. Cultivated vegetable fennel develops a large thick surface tuber, which is less developed in spice fennel. Spices like anise, caraway, cumin and dill belong to the same

plant family and are similar in form and taste. Fennel and anise have the same name in Hindi.

MYTHOLOGY: In the Middle Ages, people chewed fennel to suppress stomach noises during church services.

MEDICINAL USE: Fennel has always been regarded as a means of strengthening the body. Every mother knows that fennel relieves flatulence and stimulates milk production. Its anti-flatulence effect can be transferred through mother's milk to the baby as well. Fennel also relieves cramps and mucus in bronchitis.

PANCH PHORON

Panch phoron is a classic spice mix used in Bengali cuisine. Its unusual taste is caused by the combination of sweet fennel and bitter fenugreek with cumin, black cumin and black mustard. It is not sharp at all and is used to spice lentil and vegetable dishes.

HAVE YOU EVER TASTED IT?

SEA PERCH WITH FENNEL
Preheat an oven to 356°F . Scale and gut a 3 lb sea perch. Wash and dry the fish well. Put 2 tablespoons fennel seeds, salt and a few white pepper corns in a mortar and crush. Grease the fish with olive oil outside and then smear with the spice mix outside and inside. Bake the fish for 30 – 40 minutes, then take the fish out of the oven and put; it in a skillet. Pour 4 tablespoons Pernod over the sea perch and light on fire. When the flame goes out, flatten the fish and divide onto four plates.

IN THE KITCHEN

AROMA:
Fennel is sweet; its taste slightly resembles licorice.

USE:
In Central Europe, it is used mainly for tea or bread. It is used to season vegetable and fish dishes in Italy, southern France and China.

Five-spice mix contains fennel seeds. Fennel is used in Anglo-Saxon countries mainly as a pickling spice for cucumbers and other vegetables.

BUYING/STORING:
Fennel seeds are available in spice stores or pharmacies. They should be kept in a cool, dark place. Ground seeds must be kept in an airproof, closed container because they lose their aroma fast.

TIPS FOR COOKING:
Crushing fennel in a mortar will fully develop its aroma. In French cuisine, the leaves are used to season mayonnaises and vinaigrettes.

Fennel can be combined with parsley, oregano, sage, thyme and chili.

Illicium verum
Chinese anise

Origin:
Asia

Edible part:

Use:
✗ ♫

FAMILY: Illiciaceae

SYNONYMS: Star anise

FORMS OF USE: Fruits, whole or ground

ORIGIN: Chinese anise is native to southern China and North Vietnam. Today, it is cultivated in Cambodia, Laos, Japan and the Philippines as well.

PROPERTIES: Chinese anise is definitely a beautiful spice. It is a star-shaped fruit of an evergreen tree, which can grow up to 26 feet high and live to be more than 100 years old. It bears red-brown, corky-woody, star-shaped fruits starting from its seventh year. You can find chestnut brown, glossy, seeds inside. A single Chinese anise tree bears up to 88 lb of fruit in one year. When they are dried in the sun, they lose about three-quarters of their weight. It is not the seeds but the walls of the fruit which possess the flavor. Chinese anise is rich in essential oils, anethole in particular. It is used in food preparation and medicinally as a carminative. Chinese anise is unrelated to common anise.

RELATED SPECIES: Botanically, Chinese anise is not related to anise, but they do have similar tastes.

MYTHOLOGY: Sir Thomas Cavendish, an English navigator, brought Chinese anise from the Philippines to Plymouth on 9 September 1588. In Europe, it started as a tea spice in the court of the Russian tsar in the 17th century. Its genus name "Illicinum" is derived from the Latin word "illicere," or "attract."

MEDICINAL USE: Chew Chinese anise after eating to promote digestion and to freshen your breath. It should help with flatulence, coughing and bronchitis.

FIVE-SPICE MIX

Five-spice mix is a Chinese idea consisting of five spices mixed at fixed proportions: 1 part Chinese anise, 1 part Sezchuan pepper, ½ part cloves, ½ part cassia and 1¼ part fennel. You can buy this mix in most spice stores and the individual ingredients can be either ground or whole fruits. Five-spice mix is an essential ingredient of authentic southern Chinese and Vietnamese cuisine.

HAVE YOU EVER TASTED IT?

DUCK, CHINESE STYLE
Wash a duck in running water and pat dry. Mix 2 tablespoons five-spice mix and 4 tablespoons soy sauce and rub all over the duck. Preheat an oven to 400°F. Peel 4 garlic cloves and wash 1 bunch of spring onions. Chop finely and mix with 1 tablespoon five-spice mix, 2 tablespoons sugar and 7 tablespoons soy sauce. Fill the duck with the mix. Place the duck face down on a rack in the preheated oven and insert a pan underneath to collect fat. Roast for about 1 hour, basting the duck a few times with the collected fat.

IN THE KITCHEN

AROMA:
Chinese anise smells like anise but its taste is fuller, fiercer and deeper.

USE:
In Chinese cuisine, Chinese anise is used to spice pork, duck and goose meat. Europeans use it to spice gingerbread, stewed plums and pears and sweet dishes as well as Christmas tea and mulled wine. The oil is used instead of anise oil in candies and baked goods, ices and liquors.

BUYING/STORING:
Chinese anise is available in spice stores or in well-supplied supermarkets. Whole fruits stored in an airproof container in a dark, dry place will keep their aroma for a few years. Ground chinese anise loses its taste faster.

TIPS FOR COOKING:
Insert a piece of Chinese anise inside a chicken or duck and it will have spicy sweet aroma. Chinese anise can be combined with ginger, cinnamon, cloves, pepper and soy sauce. Besides five-spice mix, it is an ingredient in mulled wine and gingerbread spice mixes.

Juniperus communis
Juniper

Origin:

Europe, Asia

Edible part:

Use:

Property:
!

FAMILY: Cypress (*Cupressaceae*)

SYNONYMS: Juniper berry

FORMS OF USE: Berries, fresh and dry, whole and ground

ORIGIN: The juniper bush or tree grows all over Europe and in the temperate regions of Asia. The potency of the berries depends on the climate: the more sun, the more powerful the aroma. The bush bears fruit at the end of August.

PROPERTIES: Juniper is an evergreen conifer, either a tree or a bush. While the approximately 40 feet high, often columniform, trees tend to grow in lowlands, the juniper found in mountains is only 8 – 20 inches high and can live to be 2,000 years old. The trunk of old exemplars can be 3 feet thick. Its berries are green initially and turn bluish-black after one year of ripening on the tree. The berries are about 6 – 10 mm and have a wrinkled surface when dried.

RELATED SPECIES: Juniper is related to Mediterranean cypress (*Cupressus sempervirens*) and they look very much alike.

MYTHOLOGY: People believed that juniper is an intermediary between life and death and that the souls of the dead stay in a juniper tree shortly after death, symbolizing the possibility of a return to earthly life. During the Middle Ages, a widespread superstition claimed that a juniper twig could frighten devils away.

MEDICINAL USE: Juniper berries contain essential oils, such as terpineol, borneol and geramiol, which stimulate appetite, have diuretic and disinfecting properties and relax muscles. Chew the berries to suppress the symptoms of cold and flu. A juniper berry tea helps ease stomach disorders and cystitis as well as rheumatic pain.

HAVE YOU EVER TASTED IT?

GAME MARINADE
Soak a hare or a venison back or leg in a marinade for 2 days. The marinade consists of: 3 cups red wine, 5 – 6 juniper berries, 3 rosemary twigs, 10 thyme twigs, one bay leaf and black pepper corns. The game should be turned in the marinade several times.
You can use vinegar and oil instead of the red wine. In this case, only a small amount of vinegar and oil is necessary. Crush the spice in a mortar, spread onto the game and wrap the meat in a damp cloth.

IN THE KITCHEN

AROMA:
The taste of juniper is spicy and sweet, slightly reminiscent of resin. It smells similar to coniferous wood.

USE:
Juniper is a classic spice for game dishes, particularly prepared with wild swine, roe deer and pigeon. It goes well with lamb, beef and pork dishes as well as sauerkraut, red and white cabbage, beetroot and beet. Juniper is added to gin and genever (Dutch vodka).

BUYING/STORING:
This spice is available in well-stocked supermarkets. If stored in an airtight container in a cool, dark place, the berries can last up to 3 years. The spice loses its aroma fast if ground.

TIPS FOR COOKING:
Powdered or crushed juniper has the best aroma. Its taste is very strong and almost overpowering. 6 to 8 berries are sufficient for game marinade and about 4 berries are enough for sauerkraut prepared as a side dish for 4 people. Juniper is often combined with bay leaf, black pepper, mustard seeds, garlic, marjoram and thyme. Since juniper is slightly poisonous, pay close attention when measuring it. Pregnant women and people with kidney problems should avoid medicinal use of juniper.

Laserpitium siler
Sermountain

FAMILY: Carrot (*Apiaceae*)

SYNONYMS: -

FORMS OF USE: Seeds, whole or ground

ORIGIN: Sermountain is native to Asia Minor, the Caucasus and Iran. Today, it is cultivated in Turkey.

PROPERTIES: The modest plant grows wild in calcic mountainous soils. Its blossoms develop into 7 – 8 mm long and 3 – 4 mm wide seeds, which are dried after harvesting.

RELATED SPECIES: Sermountain is related and very similar to caraway and cumin.

MEDICINAL USE: Sermountain in the form of tea relieves stomachaches and dysmenorrhea and has diuretic properties.

IN THE KITCHEN

AROMA:
Sermountain has a very sharp taste and can replace pepper as well as cumin.

USE:
Sermountain is used mainly in Turkish cuisine to spice stews and dishes containing tomatoes and cabbage.

BUYING/STORING:
Sermountain is available as seeds or ground in spice stores. It should be stored in an air-proof closed container in a dark, dry place. Whole seeds keep their aroma for years if properly stored.

TIPS FOR COOKING:
You can replace sermountain with cumin.
Its whole seeds should be crushed in a mortar or roasted in a pan without any fat to develop their full aroma.
Use the spice in small quantities. Be careful not to put too much spice in a dish.

Laurus nobilis
Bay leaf

FAMILY: Laurel (*Lauraceae*)

SYNONYMS: Bay, bay laurel, true laurel, sweet bay, true bay

FORMS OF USE: Leaves, fresh and dried

ORIGIN: Bay leaf trees are native to Asia Minor and are widespread all over the Mediterranean region from Turkey to Spain as well as in Morocco. It is cultivated in the United States and in the southwestern regions of the former Soviet Union.

PROPERTIES: The evergreen tree can grow up to 50 feet high. The tree in cultivated form should be heavily pruned to enable harvesting of its leaves and twigs. In fact, many people prune it so zealously that it tends to resemble a bush. The tree has whitish-yellow blossoms, which form umbels. The blossoms develop into blue-black berries as big as hazel nuts. They are used in liquors and balms.
The dark green leaves with light green undersides are picked manually and dried in the shade. They are lanceolate and leathery.

RELATED SPECIES: The Mediterranean bay leaf is related to the Californian, West Indian and Indonesian bay leaf. These bay leaf plants are used as spices in regional cuisines.

MYTHOLOGY: The bay leaf was mentioned in a 7,000 year old Sumerian cuneiform document. Bay leaf wreaths were regarded as the symbols of victory in boxing. Roman military commanders were festooned with bay leaves if they won a battle. Bay leaves were holy for the Greeks and often offered to the god Apollo. The Greeks used bay leaves for another purpose: the priestess at Delphi prophesied with a bay leaf in her mouth. Bay leaves, if consumed in high quantities, result in trances and consciousness disorders. Charlemague recommended that bay leaves be used more as medicines and spices in Germany. Many herbalists during the Middle Ages attributed strengthening properties for the stomach and kidneys to bay leaves. Furthermore, the bay leaf was regarded as a cure for plague.

Medicinal Use: Bay leaf essences and balms are used to treat rheumatism externally and to repel insects. Oil from the berries of bay leaf trees heal sprains and contusions if used externally. Applied, externally it helps relieve flatulence in babies. Bay leaves also have antibacterial properties.

Bouquet garni

Bay leaf, parsley and thyme form the classic trio, *bouquet garni*, or "nosegay of herbs." These three herbs are usually bundled together fresh with string. You can buy it already dried and cut, a far cry from the original.

Tips for cooking

Whole leaves develop their full aroma if crushed or cut in pieces. Bay leave should be always cooked along with a dish to develop its flavor to the fullest. Scoring the leaves intensifies the flavor. Bay leaves combine excellently with juniper, black pepper and mustard seeds.

IN THE KITCHEN

AROMA:
The taste of bay leaf is acrid, aromatic, spicy and slightly bitter. Fresh leaves are extraordinarily bitter.

USE:
Everything sour goes well with bay leaves: meat aspic and cutlet aspic, sauerkraut, pickled beetroot, gherkins, mixed pickles, pickled green beans, green tomatoes and herrings. In particular, bay leaf goes well with beef, game, and fish marinades, potato dishes, roasts and all dark roast sauces, ragouts, goulashes and thick stews.

BUYING/STORING:
Dried bay leaves are available in every well-supplied supermarket. With a little luck, fresh bay leaves are available in marketplaces during the summer. Good quality bay leaves are stemless, green, dry and undamaged. A broken bay leaf loses its aroma fast. Bay leaves should be kept in a dry and dark place. Fresh leaves can be kept in the vegetable compartment of the refridgerator for weeks.

IMPORTANT WARNING:

Bay leaf, especially when drunk as a tea, can cause tipsiness in higher doses.

Levisticum officinale
Lovage

Origin:

Asia

Edible part:
🌿 🥕

Use:
✕ 🜨

Property:
❗

FAMILY: Carrot (*Apiaceae*)

SYNONYMS: Garden lovage, bladder seed, lovage angelica

FORMS OF USE: Leaves and root, fresh

ORIGIN: Lovage is probably of Central Asian origin. It was grown in the Mediterranean region at the time of the ancient Romans and has since spread throughout Europe.

PROPERTIES: The lovage plant is a perennial and can grow up to 6 feet high. It has a multi-branched rhizome, from which young plants sprout in spring and form big pinnate leaves with angular herbaceous stems and yellow umbels. The shape and taste of its leaves resemble celery. The leaves contain essential oils, tannin and bitter substances. Lovage is a Maggi spice, a fact which may suprise some people.

IN THE KITCHEN

AROMA:
Lovage smells fresh and spicy and tastes like celery.

USE:
Traditionally, lovage is used in Ligurian cuisine. The aromatic herb is increasingly popular and is used to season soups, stews, sour pickles and vinegar.

BUYING/STORING:
Lovage is available in marketplaces from May to September. Wrap it in a moist towel and store it in a bag in the refridgerator for 1 to 3 days.

TIPS FOR COOKING:
Lovage goes well with oregano, black pepper and dill.
Add the cut herb only at the end of cooking so that it will keep its aroma.

IMPORTANT WARNING:

Extremely high consumption of lovage can result in kidney disorders and dizziness. Sensitive people should reduce or avoid consumption.

Murraya koenigii
Curry leaf

Origin:

Asia

Edible part:

Use:

FAMILY: Rue (*Rutaceae*)

SYNONYMS: Ghandela, karapincha

FORMS OF USE: Leaves, fresh and dried, whole and crushed

ORIGIN: The small tree is native to India. Today, it grows wild all over the subcontinent except in the Himalayas. It even reaches Burma in the east.

PROPERTIES: This form of curry leaf resembles bay leaf. It is slightly smaller and softer, its color is olive green and its color tone changes only slightly when dried.

RELATED SPECIES: Botanically, the curry tree is related to all citrus trees. The smell of fresh curry leaf faintly resembles the aroma of tangerines.

IN THE KITCHEN

AROMA:
The taste of curry leaf is spicy and pleasantly fresh. Fresh leaves have much more intense taste than dried ones.

USE:
Curry leaf is a traditional spice in southern India and Sri Lanka. It is used to spice curries, chutneys and relishes, goes well with meat and fish dishes, and is often added to soups and stews. Curry leaf is an important ingredient in Madras curry mix.

BUYING/STORING:
The spice is available in stores selling Indian food products. Fresh leaves can be kept in a bag in the vegetable compartment of the refridgerator for a few days. Dried leaves, kept in an airtight container, will keep their aroma for months.

TIPS FOR COOKING:
If fresh curry leaf is not separated from the twig, it will keep its aroma longer.
If you have too many leaves, the best way to keep them is to deep-freeze them. Roasting, with or without fat, intensifies the aroma of curry leaf.
Curry leaf goes well with coconut milk.

Myristica fragrans
Nutmeg

Origin:

Asia

Edible part:

Use:

FAMILY: Nutmeg (*Myristicaceae*)

SYNONYMS: -

FORMS OF USE: Seeds and episperm, dried, whole and ground.

ORIGIN: The nutmeg tree is native to the Moluccas or New Guinea. Today, nutmeg is grown mainly in Indonesia, West India, Madagascar and Mauritius as well as in Brazil.

PROPERTIES: Nutmeg trees can live 100 years. In the wild, nutmeg grows up to 50 feet. Its cultivated form is pruned to a more accessible height of 20 feet to make harvesting easier. The tree only bears fruit starting from its eighth year of life and its yield increases up to the fifteenth year, when it peaks.

Nutmeg is not the fruit of the nutmeg tree: its fruit is a seed similar to apricots. The period of ripening lasts 9 months - from blooming until harvest when the tree bears fruit. The fruit is thrashed with long wooden sticks. Fruit flesh, mace or nutmeg blossom are separat-

ed and dried separately or together with the seeds (nutmeg).

MYTHOLOGY: It is hard to say how long nutmeg was known as a spice in Europe. Martius (1794–1868), a natural scientist and explorer, tried to prove that mace was known to Plautus, a Roman writer, around 200 BC, and nutmeg to scholar Pliny in about 50 AD. Nutmeg was found in Egyptian mummy graves. Thus we know that ancient peoples used nutmeg. However, it has not yet been proved whether it was used as spice or only as a medicine or for occult purposes. Nutmeg and mace belonged, besides cloves and cinnamon, among the most expensive spices during the 17th and 18th centuries.

MEDICINAL USE: Nutmeg plays an important role in folk medicine. Some people believe that if you carry it as an amulet or in a pocket, you will be protected from ulcers and boils. Nutmeg plays an important role in homeopathy even today.

RAS EL HANOUT

Ras el hanout is a North African spice mix prepared from mace, nutmeg, black pepper, cardamom, galangal, pimento, rose buds, lavender and cinnamon. You can add ginger, turmeric, black cumin, Spanish fly, cassia and fennel as well. Each Arab spice merchant has his own method of preparing this spice mix used to season rice, couscous and tangines, Tunisian or Moroccan stews.

TIPS FOR COOKING

Nutmeg is a spice best used only in pinches. Use it sparingly or the dish can taste soapy. Because nutmeg develops its aroma only when grated, it is a good idea to buy a nutmeg grater. Nutmeg loses its aroma when warmed, which is why dishes should be spiced only after cooking.

IN THE KITCHEN

AROMA:
The smell of nutmeg is pleasantly spicy; its taste is intensely spicy and slightly fiery. The taste of mace is milder. Mace can always replace nutmeg, but not vice versa.

USE:
Nutmeg is used to season everything salty: mashed potatoes and creamed spinach and cauliflower are better with a pinch of nutmeg. Thick vegetable soups, light sauces, eggs, fish and meat dishes can also be seasoned with nutmeg. Cheese fondues and eggnog are better with a pinch of nutmeg. Nutmeg is particularly good in sweet dishes like custards, puddings and stewed fruit as well as in Christmas cookies and punches.

IMPORTANT WARNING:

1 – 6 teaspoons of nutmeg can be poisonous. The substances it contains are similar to mescaline and amphetamine in a human organism and can alter consciousness and even cause death.

BUYING/STORING:
Nutmeg is available either as whole or ground nuts and mace is available either ground or as yellow brown perianth. The powder is easier to handle and thus more common. Both spices are available in well-supplied groceries and a greater selection of variations is available is spice stores. Nutmeg (as well as mace), should be kept in an airtight, closed container in a dry, dark place.

Myrrhis odorata
Cicely

Origin:

Europe

Edible part:

Use:
✗

FAMILY: Carrot (*Apiaceae*)

SYNONYMS: Sweet cicely, anise, myrrh, sweet chervil

FORMS OF USE: Seeds and leaves, fresh

ORIGIN: Cicely is native to French Savoy and is cultivated all over Europe and North America. It is grown as a garden plant in Scandinavia because it is resistant to cold.

PROPERTIES: Cicely is a perennial plant more than 3 feet high with very pinnate leaves. Its blossoms are white and form an umbel. They develop into seeds resembling fennel. The fruits are rich in essential oil, anethole in particular.

IN THE KITCHEN

AROMA:
The sweet taste of cicely is similar to licorice and its smell and taste slightly resemble a mix of fennel and anise.

USE:
The leaves of cicely are used to season salads, yogurt and cottage cheese dips. Its seeds go well with sweet dishes like custards, puddings, stewed fruits and fruit salads. Cicely has almost fallen in oblivion as a spice in some countries. However, it is still very popular in the Scandinavian region because it is easy to grow it in the garden.

BUYING/STORING:
Only fresh leaves and seeds can be used. With a little luck, both are available in summer marketplaces. Its leaves and seeds, if stored in a bag, can be kept in the vegetable compartment of the refridgerator for a few days.

TIPS FOR COOKING:
Cicely combines well with mint and sweet balm.
It absorbs acids in very sour stewed fruit like rhubarb or gooseberries and can reduce the amount of sugar. Desserts look very nice decorated with cicely as well.

Sodium chloride
Salt

Origin:
worldwide

Edible part:
All

Use:
✕ 🦞

FAMILY: Chlorides

SYNONYMS: Table salt

Forms of use: Ground in various granularity; rock salt

ORIGIN: Common salt is a common substance worldwide. Seawater is 3 percent common salt and salt is often found in underground rock salt deposits formed from ancient seas.

PROPERTIES: Sea salt, salt brine and rock salt are different. As one can recognize already from its name, sea salt is prepared of seawater or brackish water. The water evaporates in so-called salt gardens and only crystallized salt remains. Rock salt is extracted in underground salt mines. Rock salt blocks are ground and sieved. Salt brine is made of underground salt brine produced, like sea salt, by the evaporation of water. Compared to the other salts, sea salt contains other mineral and trace elements as well as sodiom.

White salt is chemically cleaned. Natural salt has grayish or brownish tinge.

MYTHOLOGY: The Romans used salt as a form of currency. The word "salary" is derived from Latin "salarium" because Roman legionaries used to collect their salary in the form of salt. Salt was very precious for a long time and was called "white gold" in colloquial speech. The state took advantage of this as well and levied salt taxes. This tax existed until 1992 in the Federal Republic of Germany, example.

Medicinal Use: Blood is a special liquid. 1 quart of human blood contains 9 g common salt. Sodium belongs among vital mineral substances. One should consume at least 2 grams of sodium chloride per day. Sodium is crucial for homeostasis in organism. Too much salt in food may cause high blood pressure in people sensitive to sodium and increase the risk of blood circulation diseases.

Types of salt and mixes

Iodized and fluoridated salt: Iodized edible salt contains potassium iodate, which supports the synthesis of calcitonin thyroxin, therefore, it can prevent goitre. 2 pounds of salt may contain not more than 25 mg of iodine. Iodized salt with fluorite contains fluoride, which helps avoid tooth decays.

Sodium-deficient salt is regarded as diet salt: Sodium can be replaced by potassium and/or magnesium. A substitution should be used by patients with high blood pressure. Its aftertaste is slightly bitter, which is why it is used less.

Spice and herbal salt: These two are mixes prepared from salt and other spices. The names of the most popular mixes are herbal salt, garlic salt, celery salt and onion salt.

IN THE KITCHEN

AROMA:
Salt tastes salty. It is hard to distinguish between sea salt, salt brine and rock salt. Iodized or fluoridated salts taste similarly as well.

USE:
A different quantity of salt is added to almost every dish. It even balances the taste of sweet dishes. It is also used for preserving.

BUYING/STORING:
Since the United States is a region lacking iodine deposits and fluorite is used to clean teeth, this salt is quite common. Overdosing on both these trace elements is impossible even when consumed in high quantities. Add a few grains of rice to a salt cellar to keep salt loose.

TIPS FOR COOKING:
1 pinch of salt should be added to each dish because it intensifies the taste of the food. It slows down the fermentation process in bread; it plays a decisive role in the aging process of cheese. Salt preserves by preventing growth of bacteria and mold on or in food.

Nigella sativa
Black cumin

FAMILY: Buttercup (*Ranunculaceae*)

SYNONYMS: Roman coriander, nutmeg flower, black caraway, fennel flower, nigella, nutmeg flower

FORMS OF USE: Seeds, dried, whole or ground

ORIGIN: Black cumin is native to eastern and southern Europe. Today, it is principally cultivated in India, Egypt and Turkey.

PROPERTIES: This annual plant grows about 24 inches high and has pinnate leaves and white-blue blossoms. The blossoms develop into perianths, which cover dark brown or black seeds. They resemble sesame seeds slightly. The seeds contain linoleic acids, oleic acids and saponin.

RELATED SPECIES: Even though the spice is called black cumin, it is not related to caraway or cumin.

MYTHOLOGY: The personal doctors of Tutankhamen treated coughing with black cumin. Cleopatra used black cumin

oil in her baths and Nefertiti used it for her complexion. The effects of black cumin were known in ancient Greece as well. Hippocrates used the natural remedy to maintain general physical or mental well-being. Black cumin is mentioned in the Old Testament. Jews season black bread with it even today. The Prophet Mohammed swore: "Black cumin heals all diseases – except for death!"

MEDICINAL USE: The unsaturated fatty acids in black cumin have a positive effect on many bodily biochemical processes. The fatty acids stabilize cell membranes and strengthen the defense of those allergic to pollen and dust, asthmatics, patients with acne and neurodermatitis. Black cumin releases mucus, improves the function of the gall bladder and stimulates menses.

HAVE YOU EVER TASTED IT?

CUCUMBER SALAD

Wash, peel and cube 1 cucumber. Put in a dish and add salt. Wash and dry 5 twigs of mint, tear leaves from herbaceous stems and cut finely. Mix with 1 teaspoon of black cumin and 1 cup Greek yogurt. Mix the yogurt sauce with the cucumbers and serve on lettuce leaves.

IN THE KITCHEN

AROMA:
Black cumin has almost no smell, but it develops an aroma when ground or chewed. Its smell slightly resembles marjoram. Its taste is aromatic and slightly bitter.

USE:
Black cumin is used mainly in Turkish, Middle Eastern and Indian cuisines. The black seeds are typically added to flat bread. However, they are also used to season vegetable dishes, salads, pickles and chutney as well as lamb and poultry dishes.

BUYING/STORING:
Corns of black cumin or ground black cumin are available in Turkish or Asian specialty stores selling foodstuffs and in spice shops. Black cumin should be stored in a cool, dark place. Corns are preferred to ground black cumin because they do not become rancid as fast.

TIPS FOR COOKING:
Black cumin develops its aroma best when crushed in a mortar or roasted in a pan without any fat.
Black cumin goes well with chili, garlic, galangal, ginger, mint, coriander and turmeric.

Ocimum basilicum
Basil

Origin:

Asia

Edible part:
🍃

Use:
✗ ♟

FAMILY: Mint (*Lamiaceae*)

SYNONYMS: Sweet basil

FORMS OF USE: Leaves, fresh and dried

ORIGIN: Basil is native to the Indian subcontinent, but basil was planted in Italy during Roman times. Basil is grown both in tropical as well as in temperate latitudes. The more intense the sunshine, the better the aroma of basil.

PROPERTIES: Basil is an annual plant with big dark green oval leaves. In late summer, the herb has white, rosy or lilac blossoms forming a spike. Basil grows up to 20 inches high. Many essential oils are responsible for its distinctive smell and taste.

RELATED SPECIES: The genus of Ocimum includes more than 60 different species. They differ in color and in the shape of the leaves. Exotic lilac forms are called "Dark Opal" or "Purple Delight." Moreover, there are lemons, cinnamon and anise basil with various aromatic nuances, as

is clear from their names. Depending on a particular cuisine, you can use either Thai basil or Mexican basil.

MEDICINAL USE: Basil has sedative effects on the nervous system. Brewed basil leaves promote sweating and help to release mucus in cold weather. Basil soothes stomach disorders, flatulence and anorexia and stimulates milk secretion in new mothers. It used to be regarded as a means to treat depression.

DID YOU KNOW …?
The name "basil" is derived from the Greek word meaning "royal." In India, basil was regarded as holy and was used in religious ceremonies. The herb was brought to central Europe by Charlemagne and was grown as a medicinal herb in cloister gardens.

HAVE YOU EVER TASTED IT?

PESTO

Wash and dry 2 bundles of basil. Tear the leaves off the herbaceous stems and cut in strip. Roast 2 tablespoons pine nuts in a pan without any fat and then cool. Peel 3 garlic cloves and mince. Put all ingredients into a high container, make a purée and add up to ⅛ cup olive oil. Mix 4 tablespoons grated Parmesan into the pesto.

IN THE KITCHEN

AROMA:
The taste of basil is sweetly spicy and pleasantly peppery. It gives dishes a fresh aroma.

USE:
Basil is a classic spice of Italian cuisine. Pesto, insalada caprese and pizza margherita are not complete without this spice. Basil goes well with salads, vegetable dishes and dips.

BUYING/STORING:
Basil is available either fresh or dried in every supermarket. It is better to buy fresh basil with roots because it is more flavorful and lasts longer. Dry basil has a less intense and slightly harsh aroma. It will keep if stored in an airtight, closed container in a dark, cool place.

TIPS FOR COOKING:
Add basil only shortly before the end of cooking or it will lose its aroma.

Basil can be used to garnish soups and salads.

Fresh basil can be cut finely, mixed with little water and frozen into ice cubes to be added to dishes.

Origanum majorana
Marjoram

Origin:

Asia

Edible part:
🌿

Use:
✗ ♫

FAMILY: Mint (*Lamiaceae*)

SYNONYMS: Majorana hortensis, knotted marjoram, sweet marjoram

FORMS OF USE: Leaves, fresh and dried

ORIGIN: Marjoram is native to the eastern Mediterranean region. However, it has been used all over the Mediterranean region since ancient times. It is cultivated mainly in Spain and France as well as in Germany. The more intense the sunshine, the better the aroma.

PROPERTIES: Marjoram is a perennial plant. It is not cold resistant and, therefore, it is known as an annual plant in cooler latitudes. The plant is 8 – 24 inches high with square herbaceous stems and ovate, rounded, pilous leaves. Marjoram can be easily recognized by its velvety gray and white-lilac blossoms. Essential oils, terpene, bitter substances and tannin influence its scent and taste. The plant is harvested shortly before its blossoms open.

RELATED SPECIES: Although marjoram and oregano are closely related, they do not harmonize at all. There are multiple variants (like wild marjoram) of majoram as well.

MYTHOLOGY: The Egyptians, Greeks and Romans used marjoram to spice their wine in the hope of increasing their potency. The Greeks sacrificed marjoram as "incense" in honor of Aphrodite. The name "marjoram" is probably derived from the Arabic *marjamie*, or 'incomparable.'

MEDICINAL USE: Medieval herbalists believed almost all maladies ranging from rings under the eyes, to asthma and physical pains to pulmonary tuberculosis could be healed with marjoram. Today, marjoram is regarded as a means of strengthening the stomach. Because it promotes digestion, it is good to add marjoram to fatty dishes like goose and lard.

HAVE YOU EVER TASTED IT?

HEAVENLY APPLE BED

Dice 2 onions and sauté them in butter until they turn glassy, cube 10 oz dry sausage and add it to the onion and cook. Peel 1 lb apples, core and cut into thick slices and sauté in butter in a separate pan. Add 3 tablespoons raisins, honey and salt and pepper. Wash one twig of marjoram tear off the leaves and cut finely. Put the apple mixture onto a plate, place the roasted dry sausage on top and garnish with marjoram.

IN THE KITCHEN

AROMA:
The taste of marjoram is spicy, slightly acrid and very aromatic. Its smell is very intense.

USE:
Marjoram is traditionally added to smoked foods. It goes well with white beans, pea soup, potato soup, sourkraut, ground meat, mutton and pork, meat paste and goose filling. Marjoram improves the taste of salads, various vegetable dishes, cheese dishes, dumplings and baked potatoes as well.

BUYING/STORING:
Dried and sometimes even fresh marjoram is readily available in supermarkets. Fresh marjoram should be wrapped in a moist towel and put into a bag. It can be kept in the vegetable compartment of the refridgerator for 3 – 4 days. Dry marjoram should be kept in an airtight container in a dark, cool place.

TIPS FOR COOKING:
Marjoram goes well with thyme, bay leaf and juniper. It should be added to dishes shortly before they are finished cooking.

Origanum vulgare
Oregano

Origin:

Europe

Edible part:
🌿

Use:
✕ 𝕬

FAMILY: Mint (*Lamiaceae*)

SYNONYMS: Pot marjoram, wild marjoram, winter sweet, European oregano, organy

FORMS OF USE: Leaves, fresh and dried

ORIGIN: Oregano is native to the Mediterranean region and can be grown all over mid latitudes. The more intense the sunshine, the better the aroma.

PROPERTIES: Oregano is a bushy herb with many leaves. It grows up to 24 inches high. Its many ovate, pointed leaves are ½ – 1 inch long. Light pink or whitish, bell-shaped calyxes form false spikes in the shape of heads. The smell and taste derive from the essential oils carvacrol and thymol.

RELATED SPECIES: Oregano and marjoram are close relatives. However, they do not combine well at all.
Mexican oregano is a very distant relative of European oregano, although they taste very similar. The plant (*Lippia graveolens*) is closely related to the locally cultivated lemon verbena.

MYTHOLOGY: Oregano is said to be a symbol of joy inspired by Aphrodite, the Greek goddess of love. Brides and grooms were festooned with oregano wreathes because the herb was considered a sure means to strengthen the love between two people.

MEDICINAL USE: Oregano is used to relieve flatulence, diarrhea and stomachache in folk medicine. It stimulates the appetite and soothes dysmenorrhia, laryngitis and pharyngitis. Oregano has disinfecting and antibacterial properties, which are used mainly to treat coughing and histoplasmosis.

PIZZA SPICE MIX

Oregano is the main ingredient of pizza spice mix. The spice contains a mix of paprika, pepper, thyme or salt and chili as well. Pizza spice mixes should be kept in an air-proof, closed container. They are predominantly used to season pizzas and pasta sauces.

HAVE YOU EVER TASTED IT?

RUMP STEAK WITH TOMATO AND MOZZARELLA

Fry both sides of 2 rumps in a pan with a little olive oil and season with salt and coarsely ground pepper. Wash, dry and slice 1 tomato. Slice mozzarella. Wash 2 twigs of fresh oregano, dry and mince. Garnish both underdone steaks with the tomato slices, season with oregano and cover with mozzarella. Cover the pan with a lid and cook until the cheese melts. Serve on toasted bread – a perfect dish!

IN THE KITCHEN

AROMA:
The taste of oregano is spicy, slightly sweet and pleasantly fresh. It has an intense smell.

USE:
Oregano is classic spice to season pizza and pasta. It goes well with vegetable dishes made from pumpkins, zucchini, peppers and potatos and as well as with pork and beef roasts.

BUYING/STORING:
Oregano is available either dried or sometimes fresh in supermarkets. Oregano should be wrapped in a moist towel and put into a bag in the vegetable compartment of the refridgerator for 3 – 4 days. The aroma of dried oregano is very strong. It should be kept in an airtight, closed container in a dark, cool place.

TIPS FOR COOKING:
Oregano goes well with rosemary and thyme. However, it does not go well with marjoram, its close relative.
Dried oregano is an aromatic spice and should be added into dishes shortly before the end of cooking so that it can fully develop its aroma.
In Mexico oregano is mixed with chili powder and used to season chili con carne.

Papaver somniferum
Poppy

Origin:

Asia

Edible part:

Use:

Property:

!

FAMILY: Poppy (*Papaveraceae*)

SYNONYMS: Opium poppy, white poppy

FORMS OF USE: Seeds, dried, whole or ground

ORIGIN: The opium poppy is native to Asia Minor and the Mediterranean region. It is difficult to find out its exact origin owing to its early cultivation during the Neolithic Age. Today, opium poppies are grown mainly in Turkey, Greece and India as well as in Holland and Germany. Opium poppies are relatively new in Europe.

PROPERTIES: This annual, 28 – 47 inches high herb has blue-green leaves and white, violet-red blossoms. The blossoms develop into walnut sized-pods containing blue-gray round poppy seeds. Poppy seeds are rich in linoleic acids and contain, contrary to the herb juice, few opiates.

RELATED SPECIES: Opium poppy is related to corn poppy, which is less poisonous.

MYTHOLOGY: The Greek goddess Demeter is always depicted carrying poppy flowers in her hand. Opium, or "poppy tears," has been used in the Mediterranean region since about the 3rd or 4th century BC. The extract from the leaves of the poppy plant was usually called meconium. Dioscorides and Pliny precisely described both the preparation and effects of opium. The British waged two wars in China because the Chinese wanted to prohibit the export of opium made from poppy juice.

MEDICINAL USE: Opiates were used as painkillers in medicine. The Greeks and the Romans used poppy juice as a soporific drug. The genus name "Papaver" is probably derived from the Latin "papa," or 'children's pap' because poppy was added to the milk of upset children to calm them down. The species name "somniferum" refers to its soporific effect (Lat. somniferum = soporific).

Sift two cups flour into a bowl and make a depression in the center. Add 1 packet of dried yeast and 7 tablespoons sugar. Put a pinch of salt, 2 eggs and 1 cup lukewarm milk in the bowl and prepare smooth dough with the mixing wisk of a food processor. Cover and let rise in a warm place until doubled in volume. To prepare the filling, mix ½ a cup sugar, ½ cup poppy seeds and ½ cup milk and simmer for about 5 minutes. Add 7 tablespoons raisins and a little grated lemon peel. Knead the dough on a rolling board covered with cornmeal and roll into a rectangle 12 x 16 inches. Spread the filling over it. Roll the dough from the longer side. Butter a baking sheet and sprinkle with flour. Put the roll on the baking sheet and brush with milk. Make zigzag notches on the surface with a knife. Cover the poppy twist and let it sit for about 1 hour. Then bake it in the lower part of a pre-heated oven at 400°F for about 45 minutes.

IN THE KITCHEN

AROMA:
Poppy seeds do not smell. They have taste similar to nuts and are slightly acrid.

USE:
In most European cuisines, poppy seeds are used for baking. They go well with piquant baked goods like rolls, bread and crackers as well as with sweet dishes like cakes, strudels, twists and yeast dumplings. White poppy is used mainly in Indian cuisine to season chutney and sauces.

BUYING/STORING:
Poppy seeds are available in the bakery ingredients section in every well-supplied grocery. They should be kept in a cool, dry place. Whole corn or ground seeds can be used for baking. If you do not own a poppy seed grinder, try to find canned poppy seed filling.

TIPS FOR COOKING:
Poppy seeds should be ground in a special poppy seed grinder to best develop their aroma.

IMPORTANT WARNING:

Although poppy seeds are not poisonous, they do contain a small amount of opiates. Therefore, small children should not eat too much poppy cake.

Pimenta dioica
Allspice

Origin:

America

Edible part:

Use:

Property:

!

FAMILY: Myrtaceae

SYNONYMS: Jamaican pepper, piment, pimento

FORMS OF USE: Seeds, dried, whole or ground

ORIGIN: The allspice tree is native to and cultivated in Central America and the West Indian Islands. The best allspice is supposedly grown in Jamaica, which is responsible for almost two thirds of the world's supply.

PROPERTIES: The evergreen allspice tree is 20 – 40 feet high and lives to be 100 years old. It bears its first fruit during the seventh year. The yield of an allspice tree can reach about 100 lbs in a good year. Its berries develop from little, white blossoms which are picked before ripening. The berries are fermented and dried with wrinkled, skinny, brown skins. The aroma is influenced by essential oils, eugenol in particular.

RELATED SPECIES: Botanically, the allspice tree is closely related to the clove tree.

MYTHOLOGY: The Aztecs and the Mayans were familiar with this spice. They used it for occult purposes and also to season chocolate.

MEDICINAL USE: Allspice oil is said to relieve colic and flatulence; crushed and cooked seeds spread on a cloth and put on a painful place should help rheumatism and neuralgia.

NUREMBERG GINGERBREAD

Cut 7 tablespoons dried apricots in pieces. Heat ¾ cup beet syrup and add 3½ tablespoons brown sugar, 2 tablespoons oil and 2 tablespoons water in a pot. Cool. Add 1 egg yolk, 1 teaspoon cocoa, 1 teaspoon grated lemon peel, 1 pinch of ground allspice and ½ teaspoon ground cinnamon. Add 1 cup flour, 2 teaspoons natron, 5½ tablespoons ground hazelnuts and 5½ tablespoons ground almonds as well as 3½ tablespoons orange and apricot cubes to the dough. Preheat the oven to 350°F. Roll out the dough to thick rounds and place them on a baking sheet covered with baking paper. Bake in the middle of the oven for about 15 minutes. Make frosting from 1 cup powdered sugar, 1 egg white and 2 tablespoons lemon juice. Cool the gingerbread and then spread with the frosting.

IN THE KITCHEN

AROMA:
The smell of allspice is similar to cloves with a shade of cinnamon and nutmeg. Its taste is peppery sharp.

USE:
Allspice berries are used to season marinades for game, beef and fish. Gherkins, mixed pickles and cabbage dishes, game pate and saverkraut are better with a little allspice. Liquors like Stonsdorfer, Chartreuse and Benedictine also contain allspice extracts.

IMPORTANT WARNING:

Pregnant women should neither apply allspice oil nor use the spice as an air freshener. It can cause miscarriage.

BUYING/STORING:
Allspice is available whole or ground in every well-supplied grocery. The berries last up to 3 years if properly stored; the powder loses its aroma fast. Therefore, keep allspice in an airtight container in a dry, dark place.

TIPS FOR COOKING:
The full aroma develops only when allspice is crushed in a mortar or ground in a grinder. Allspice goes well with nutmeg, clove and pepper as well as with lemon and vinegar.

Pimpinella anisum
Anise

Origin:

Asia

Edible part:

Use:

FAMILY: Carrot (*Apiaceae*)

SYNONYMS: Anis

FORMS OF USE: Seeds, dried, whole or ground

ORIGIN: Anise plant is native to Asia and was cultivated in Mediterranean countries in ancient times. Since anise needs sunlight, the plant is grown mainly in southern European countries as well as in India and Central and South America.

PROPERTIES: The anise plant grows up to 24 inches tall and has round leaves. Double schizocarpic fruits develop from umbels with white blossoms. Seeds are 3 – 6 mm long, about 2 mm wide and slightly falciform. Depending on the place of origin, they are either light green or gray-brownish. When ripe, the plant is cut and thrashed. The seeds may be dried as well.

RELATED SPECIES: Botanically, anise is closely related to fennel, caraway, coriander and dill.

MYTHOLOGY: Anise was recognized as a spice and a medical product 3,500 years ago. The Egyptians used its leaves and seeds. Anise spread over the Mediterranean region and even reached Central and northern Europe thanks to the monks during the reign of Charlemagne. Munching on a few corns of anise after eating a big meal was a widespread custom in the Orient. The Romans ate a special anise cake as a dessert to freshen their breath and to aid digestion. In ancient times, anise seeds were used in cosmetics. Anise was said to increase potency as well.

MEDICINAL USE: Anise stimulates the production of bile and helps digestion after eating fatty dishes. It also relieves flatulence, colic and coughing fits. It releases mucus, strengthens the heart and respiratory organs and relaxes the nerves. Anise assists in breastmilk production. Anise oil repels lice and mosquitoes. Its essential oils cause muscle paralysis in parasites.

HAVE YOU EVER TASTED IT?

ANISE MACAROONS

Preheat an oven 200°F. Beat 2 egg whites with an electric whisk at maximum speed. Gradually add 7 tablespoons fine sugar. Add 3 tablespoons chemically untreated grated lemon peel and 1 teaspoon ground anise to the beaten whites. Pour the mixture into a pastry bag with a star-shaped tip and squeeze small mounds onto a baking sheet covered with baking paper. Bake in the middle of an oven for about 1½ hours. Cool on a cake rack.

IN THE KITCHEN

AROMA:
The smell of anise is pleasantly sweet and aromatic. The taste of the spice is piquant and fresh.

USE:
Anise is used to season Christmas sweets as well as bread and cakes. Sweet dishes like fruit salads, stewed apples and pears, milk and semolina dishes and plum jam are enhanced with anise as well. Liquors like pastis, anise liquor, ouzo, arrack, Pernod, Ricard and sambuca have aromas similar to licorice because they contain anise.

BUYING/STORING:
Anise is available as whole seeds or ground in well-supplied groceries. If kept in an air-proof container in a dry, cool, dark place, anise will keep its aroma for about 1 year.

TIPS FOR COOKING:
Before using, anise seeds should be crushed in a mortar to bring out their full aroma.

Anise can be overpowering. Be very careful when using it in cooking and baking.

Anise does not combine well with other very aromatic spices. It is best used alone.

Piper nigrum
Black pepper

Origin:

Asia

Edible part:

Use:

✗

Property:

❗

FAMILY: Pepper (*Piperaceae*)

SYNONYMS: Madagascar pepper, common pepper

FORMS OF USE: Fruit (pickled, dried and ground)

ORIGIN: Pepper is native to the monsoon forests of India. It is cultivated mainly in India, Indonesia, Malaysia and Brazil.

PROPERTIES: Pepper grows in the form of berries on an evergreen climbing plant. A wild plant reaches a height of 30 feet, while cultivated varieties are bred to reach only 13 feet in order to make harvest easier. A pepper bush is completely mature when it is about 8 years old. It bears fruit for about 20 years. Spadix-like inflorescences develop into fruits resembling red currants. Depending on the degree of ripeness, berries are green or red. They are picked in various stage of ripening, according to personal preference, and processed further. Alkaloid piperine is responsible for its hot taste.

MEDICINAL USE: Because of its sharp flavor, pepper warms up the body, boosting the metabolism and helping digestion by stimulating salivation and digestive juices. Pepper increases appetite and eases flatulence. Piperin contained in pepper is used in some stomach tonics and stomach medicines.

DID YOU KNOW ...?

Besides salt, pepper corns are the most popular and common spice in most households. Pepper is relatively cheap today, but this has not always been the case. The ancient Greeks knew that pepper stimulates the appetite. During Roman times, pepper was a sign of wealth and prestige because its sharp flavor only seasoned meals in rich households. In ancient Rome, successful merchants who traded spices were called "pepper bags." During the Middle Ages, pepper was weighed in gold. Since pepper is native to countries in the Far East faraway from Europe, an insult developed among Europeans: "Go where pepper grows!"

PEPPER SPECIES

Green pepper is an unripe harvested corn generally pickled in salt or vinegar brine or freeze-dried using a special procedure immediately after being harvested. Green pepper is very aromatic and there are many ways to use it. Pickled vegetables receive a special flavor from this mild pepper. However, it is good to use it in meat dishes that cook for a long time like game, lamb or pork roast. Since green pepper is soft, it can be used for pastes, marinades and spreads. Strawberries with green pepper is a unique culinary experience.

Black pepper is an unripe harvested green berry which is dried in the sun after being picked. It becomes black and hardens. The spice is sharp and fiery. Use black pepper in sauces, soups and marinades, roasted and grilled meat, ragouts and stews as well as in game, meat fillings and pasta dishes.

White pepper is a red, fully ripe harvested berry that is soaked for about one week before its skin is removed. Then the corns are dried in the sun and gain their distinctive yellow-white color. Since it is finer and milder than the other types of pepper, it complements salads, spicy cottage cheese dishes, light sauces and fish very nicely.

Long pepper belongs to the pepper family as well. It is a tropical climbing plant with about 1 inch long, cone-shaped ears which turn light brown when dried. It is as sharp as black pepper, but its taste is simultaneously slightly sweet and sour. Grind or crush in a mortar before using.

Red pepper grows on Brazilian pepper trees all over South America. Fully ripe pink berries are not processed in the same way as black pepper. Its taste is sweet, spicy and only slightly sharp.

IMPORTANT WARNING:

Use red pepper sparingly and keep containers containing it away from children. It is poisonous when eaten in large qualitities.

TIPS FOR COOKING

Two ground rules: Put white pepper in light dishes, black pepper in dark dishes. Cook whole pepper corns in the dish the whole time. When using ground pepper, add it only at the end of cooking.

Biting into a pepper corn can be unpleasant. Therefore, cook pepper corns in a little textile bag or in a tea ball and remove it from the dish before serving.

IN THE KITCHEN

AROMA:
Pepper does not smell at all and its taste is sharp and slightly hot.

USE:
Next to salt, pepper is a universal spice in European and North American cuisines. It is used to season all savory dishes. Moreover, green pepper seasons sweet desserts like fruit salad, strawberries and chocolate dishes as well.
Black pepper is a part of many spice mixes such as curry and *quatre épices*. It is also used to produce pepper oil essence for perfume.

BUYING/STORING:
Pepper is available whole or ground in every grocery. If kept in a cool, dark place in an air-proof container, pepper corns should last up to 3 years. An open jar of green pepper corns should be stored in a fridge and will last about 4 – 6 weeks.

Rhus coriaria
Sumac

FAMILY: Sumac (*Anacardiaceae*)

SYNONYMS: Sicilian sumach, sumac, elm-leaved sumach, tanner's sumach

FORMS OF USE: fruits, dried, whole or ground

ORIGIN: The sumach bush grows wild all over the Mediterranean region. It is particularly common in Iran, Turkey, Syria and Lebanon.

PROPERTIES: Sumach consists of dried red fruits of a bush up to 10 feet high. They develop from small yellow blossoms forming a panicle. Light red branches and leaves are pilous. After harvesting, the fruits are dried and ground. They contain tannin and fruit acids.

MEDICINAL USE: Sumach can be used to staunch bleeding and to relieve diarrhea.

In the Kitchen

Aroma:
Sumach tastes slightly sour, acrid and refreshing.

Use:
Sumach is a popular spice in Syrian, Lebanese and Turkish cuisines. Kebabs and other grilled meat, poultry and fish are seasoned with it in most countries. In powder form, it is added to yogurt dips and dusted onto salads. It is used to spice rice and legumes.

Buying/storing:
Sumach is available in dry and ground form in Turkish groceries and spice stores. It should be kept closed in an airproof container in a cool, dark place.

Tips for cooking:
To prepare a slightly sour marinade for grilling poultry, pour hot water over the powder or the berries and cool.

Rosmarinus officinalis
Rosemary

Origin:

Europe

Edible part:

Use:

FAMILY: Mint (*Lamiaceae*)

SYNONYMS: romero, alecrim

FORMS OF USE: Leaves, fresh and dried

ORIGIN: Rosemary is native to the Mediterranean region where it grows wild even today. It is cultivated in Spain, France, North Africa and the United States. Rosemary likes sun and does not like too much water. The more intense the sunshine, the better the aroma.

PROPERTIES: Rosemary is an evergreen plant which is not frost-resistant. It can grow up to 5 feet high, but it is usually merely a knee-high bush. The narrow, blue-green leaves smell like resin and are shaped like fir needles. Rosemary has little lilac blossoms. The taste and aroma are affected by its essential oils, tannin, bitter substances, resins, flavonoides and saponins.

MYTHOLOGY: Rosemary was regarded as a holy herb by the ancient Egyptians, Greeks and Romans. It was a sym-

bol of fidelity and was supposed to improve memory and thus symbolized the constancy of lovers. In ancient Greece, students wore wreaths of rosemary to support their ability to learn. Rosemary was said to chase away ghosts. It was burnt in invalids' rooms to clear the air. During the Plague, people wore sachets filled with rosemary around their necks to ward off infection.

MEDICINAL USE: Rosemary balances nerves and blood circulation, relieves exhaustion, stomach aches and headaches, soothes rheumatism, neuritis and cramps, and stimulates bile and digestive juice production.

DID YOU KNOW …?

"Ros" and "marinus" mean, respectively, "dew" and "sea" in Latin. Rosemary is devoted to the goddess of love and beauty, Aphrodite, and was regarded as a symbol of fertility. A twig of rosemary was placed in cradles and worn as a wedding wreath. Courting couples planted a rosemary twig in hopes of a long and happy marriage.

HAVE YOU EVER TASTED IT?

ROSEMARY OIL

Put 3 – 4 twigs of fresh rosemary in a sterilized 2 cup jar and fill it with quality oil (olive oil for instance). The oil will take on the aroma of rosemary in about 2 weeks. You can enhance the flavor of the oil with a peeled garlic clove, a little allspice and some pepper corns.

ROSEMARY VINEGAR

To prepare rosemary vinegar, put a few twigs into a sterilized jar. To prepare mild vinegar, warm it for a short time and pour white wine or sherry vinegar over the twigs until they are covered. Strain the vinegar for about 3 weeks. Use it to season salads or basting.

IN THE KITCHEN

AROMA:
The taste of rosemary is resiny and spicy. Fresh rosemary is very aromatic. If dried, its taste is slightly bitter and acrid and should be used sparingly.

USE:
Rosemary is a classic spice of Mediterranean cuisine. However, it is used in Central European cuisines as well to season lamb, game, pork and poultry. It goes well with fruits and vegetables like tomatoes, pumpkins, zucchini as well as with string beans, potatoes and legumes.

BUYING/STORING:
Rosemary is available either fresh or dried in every supermarket. Fresh rosemary twigs should be wrapped in a moist towel and put in a bag in the refridgerator. If you intend to store them for more than 1 week, however, freeze them. Dried rosemary should be kept in an airtight container in a dark, cool place.

TIPS FOR COOKING:
Rosemary should be added to dishes early. Remove the twigs before serving. Fresh rosemary twigs can be used as skewers to pierce meat and vegetables for kebabs.
Rosemary goes well with garlic and thyme.

Ruta graveolens
Common rue

Origin:

Europe

Edible part:

Use:

Property:

!

FAMILY: Rue (*Rutaceae*)

SYNONYMS: Herb-of-grace

FORMS OF USE: Leaves (fresh and dried)

ORIGIN: Common rue is a typical plant from Macchia in the Mediterranean region. It is not absolutely clear whether the Romans or only the medieval Benedictines used common rue first.

PROPERTIES: Common rue is a forb about 20 inches high. Its leaves are pinnate and gray-brown. The plant has little yellow blooms forming a panicle. A range of essential oils, tannin and bitter substances as well as resin are responsible for its aroma.

MEDICINAL USE: Common rue mitigates eye diseases and headache. Alternative medicine recommends it for phlebitis.

In the kitchen

Aroma:
Common rue tastes spicy, slightly sour and bitter.

Use:
If used sparingly, it can be used to season salads, meat and cheese dishes, legumes, spinach, cabbage and mushrooms as well as fish. It is a classic ingredient in grappas as well.

Buying/storing:
Dried common rue is available only in pharmacies. If you want the herb fresh, you should grow it yourself in a garden because it is seldom available in marketplaces. Keep dried common rue in a dark, dry place. If keeping for a few days, wrap fresh common rue in a moist towel and keep it in a bag in the vegetable compartment of the refridgerator.

Tips for cooking:
Use common rue with care because its taste is very intense. Crush dried common rue in a mortar or pour a little hot water over it to develop its full aroma.

Important warning:

Even in small amounts, common rue can cause allergic responses in sensitive people. High quantities of rue can cause digestive problems and can even be poisonous. Pregnant women should avoid consuming it because it can cause miscarriage.

Salvia officinalis
Sage

Origin:

Europe

Edible part:

Use:

✗ ♨

Property:

❗

FAMILY: Mint (*Lamiaceae*)

SYNONYMS: Common sage, ramona, sage, sauge

FORMS OF USE: Leaves, fresh and dried

ORIGIN: Sage is native to the Mediterranean region, but it has bean spread over Central Europe, and even Asia Minor, since the 9th century.

PROPERTIES: Common sage is a perennial forb growing up to 32 inches high with gray-green, oval and slightly pilous leaves on woody shoots and light blue or light lilac blossoms in July. Its spicy-bitter leaves are used for seasoning. They are rich in essential oils and thujone and smell very aromatic.

RELATED SPECIES: There are hundreds of sage species. The most common relatives of sage are: pineapple sage (*salvia rutilans*), cherry sage (*salvia greggii*), grapefruit sage (*salvia dorisiana*), and clary sage (*salvia sclarea*), which is cultivated for use in the perfume industry because of its

intense nutmeg smell. All the listed species are similar to divine sage (*salvia divinorum*), which is native to Central America. The latter was a sacrificial herb of the Central American indigenous peoples.

MYTHOLOGY: The medicinal power of sage was appreciated first by the ancient Romans. It was grown in cloister gardens in the time of Charlemague. A verse from the 13th century credits sage with warding off death and for a long time, occult powers were attributed to it. Sage was first used in cooking during the Middle Ages.

MEDICINAL USE: Sage has anti-inflammatory, painkilling and perspiratory properties. Because of its anti-inflammatory function, it is suitable for soothing gingivitis and as mouth wash. It calms stomach viruses and can prevent light influenza infections. It also prevents lactation. Furthermore, a cup of sage tea on hot summer days is very pleasant.

HAVE YOU EVER TASTED IT?

SALTIMBOCCA
8 tender, little veal steaks, 2 oz each. Garnish with 1 sage leaf and 1 slice of air-dried, raw ham. Fix with toothpicks. Heat 2 tablespoons of margarine in a pan, cook the saltimbocca and turn after 3 – 4 minutes. Take it out of the pan and keep warm. Baste the dripping with ½ cup veal broth and 1 glass of white wine. Cook and season the sauce with a pinch of salt and black pepper. Serve 2 saltimbocca and a little sauce on each plate. It goes well with wide pasta.

In the Kitchen

Aroma:
The taste of salvia is fresh, spicy, slightly bitter and almost soapy if used in excess.

Use:
Sage is a classic spice in Italian cuisine. Classic dishes include saltimbocca, tortellini with sage butter and polenta with gorgonzola and sage. It seasons tomatoes, potatoes, greens, minced meat and poultry stulfings very well.

Buying/storing:
Sage is available fresh and dried in every supermarket. Fresh sage twigs should be wrapped in a moist towel and put in a bag stored in the vegetable compartment of the refridgerator. Dried sage has more intense aroma than fresh salvia. It should be stored in an airtight container in a dark, cool place.

Tips for cooking:
Sage goes well with rosemary, thyme, oregano, parsley and bay leaf. Use sage with care – it can be overpowering. Roast salvia in oil to bring out its full aroma.

Important warning:

Thujone eaten in large amounts is poisonous. Severe nervous diseases develop if used often in high quantities.

Sassafras albidum
Sassafras

FAMILY: Laurel (*Lauraceae*)

SYNONYMS: -

FORMS OF USE: Leaves and bark (dried)

ORIGIN: The sassafras tree is native to North America. It grows in deciduous mixed forests near the North American Atlantic coast. The tree is not known on any other continent.

PROPERTIES: The sassafras tree grows about 43 feet high. Its leaves are lobate and are about 7 inches long. Its blossoms are yellow and develop into dark berries, but they should not be consumed. The taste is affected by essential oils such as safrole.

MYTHOLOGY: Sassafras is holy for the indigenous American peoples, for whom it symbolizes love. Sassafras can have hallucinogenic and aphrodisiacal effects.

In the Kitchen

Aroma:
Sassafras tastes spicy, but not hot.

Use:
Sassafras is the spice of classic southern cuisine in the United States and is especially popular in Louisiana. It refines gumbos, a Creole stew prepared from seafood, fish and poultry and even vegetable stews.

Buying/storing:
Sassafras is available mainly as powder and only in spice stores. Depending on whether the leaves are ground, it is gray-greenish or light brown. The powder should be kept in an airtight container in a dry, dark place.

Tips for cooking:
Add sassafras to warm, not boiling dishes or the spice will release its fibers. It thickens dishes slightly.
Sassafras goes well with chili, coriander and parsley.

Important warning:

In higher doses, sassafras works as a nerve poison because it contains safrole.

Satureja hortensis
Savory

Origin:

Asia

Edible part:

Use:

FAMILY: Mint (*Lamiaceae*)

SYNONYMS: Summer savory, sedree, ajedra

FORMS OF USE: Leaves (fresh and dried)

ORIGIN: Savory is native from the eastern Mediterranean region to Iran. Today, it is cultivated in all Mediter-ranean countries, Central Europe, western Asia and India as well as in southern Africa and North America.

PROPERTIES: Savory is an annual, shrubby plant which grows up to 20 inches high. Its paired leaves are dark green, lanceolate. They are about 1 inch long and ⅛ inch wide and have very thin barbs on the edge. The blossoms of savory are pink or light lilac. The herb is cut before blooming, when its flavor and aroma are most pungent. Savory gets along both in a flowerpot with beans and in a garden. It can even act as a natural pesticide. String beans, for example, are almost free from greenflies if savory is planted nearby.

RELATED SPECIES: Perennial winter savory (Satureja montana) is a close relative. Its taste is slightly more acrid than the taste of summer savory.

MYTHOLOGY: The ancient Romans used savory as a cooking spice and medicinal herb. They also believed in its powers as an aphrodisiac. This knowledge was noted in medieval medical documents prescribing it to ensure fidelity in marriage.

MEDICINAL USE: Savory promotes digestion and strengthens the stomach. It relieves coughing and obstruction of airways with mucus. Savory acts as an antiseptic for pharynx and larynx injuries.

Have you ever tasted it?

Turkish bean soup
Wash and dry 1 lb young, wide string beans and cut into 1 inch long pieces. Peel and mince 1 onion and 2 garlic cloves. Wash, dry and cut up 1 lb lamb leg. Heat 2 tablespoons olive oil in a pot and sauté the cubes of meat with onion and garlic. Add the beans and 1 quart vegetable broth. Spice with 5 twigs of savory, 1 twig of rosemary, 5 twigs of thyme, a pinch of salt and pepper. Cook everything at medium temperature for about 40 minutes. Scrape out the flesh of 2 tomatoes, boil briefly, cool and peel off the skin. Quarter the tomatoes and remove the herbaceous stems and grains and chop. Add the tomatoes to the soup and simmer for 5 minutes. Remove the herb twigs from the stew and season.

IN THE KITCHEN

AROMA:
The taste of savory is peppery, slightly hot and smells very spicy.

USE:
Savory is an attractive ingredient because it reduces flatulence. It goes well with fatty meat, game and fish dishes, heavy soups, baked potatoes, potato and bean salads as well as tomato and mushroom dishes. It can be used as a seasoning for smoked foods.

BUYING/STORING:
Savory is available in some marketplaces where one can buy it with fresh beans. Its fresh form is available only in marketplaces, but its dried form is available in well-supplied supermarkets or spice stores. Keep fresh leaves in the vegetable compartment of the refridgerator. Dried savory should be kept in an airtight container in a dark, cool place.

TIPS FOR COOKING:
Fresh savory can be frozen and dried. Use savory with care. Its full aroma is brought out during cooking.
Add whole fresh savory to dishes and remove before serving.

Sesam indicum
Sesame

Origin:

Asia

Edible part:

Use:

FAMILY: Sesame (*Pedaliaceae*)

SYNONYMS: Gingelly, benne

FORMS OF USE: Seeds (dried, whole or ground)

ORIGIN: Sesame belongs among the oldest cultivated plants in the world. It originated in Mesopotamia between the Euphrates and the Tigris, and in India and Africa a thousand years ago. Sesame spread to China, Japan and the Mediterranean countries. It is cultivated in Turkey, India, China, Ecuador, Honduras, Nicaragua, and Mexico today.

PROPERTIES: A sesame plant has long, straight up to 6 feet high herbaceous stems with long, oval leaves. Its blossoms are white or wine red and resemble foxglove. Seeds are ripe 12 weeks after sowing. They are found in long pods and are about 2 mm. The plant is cut and dried in bundles. The pods open slowly and sesame falls out, hence the expression: "Open sesame!"

Sesame is composed of, depending on its particular form, up to 50 percent oil, which consists almost of several fold unsaturated fatty acids, 20 – 40 percent protein and a significant amount of vitamin E, lecithin and niacin. Moreover, it is rich in calcium, iron and magnesium.

MEDICINAL USE: Sesame has detoxifying as well as laxative functions. It promotes menses and prevents hair loss and headaches. Because of its high content of calcium and essential fatty acids, it is recommended for osteoporosis prophylaxis. Sesame oil is used in traditional Asiatic medicine as well as in massage oil and is supposed to aid in relaxation.

Tahini

Tahini is a paste prepared from ground sesame. It is available either with or without salt in natural food stores, shops selling dietetic products or in Arab groceries. The paste is used to spice meat and vegetable dishes in Oriental cuisine. Spread on bread as a healthy, exotic and delicious alternative to salami or marmalade.

Gomasio

Gomasio, also known as sesame salt, is a mix of roasted, ground sesame and sea salt. It has been used as a traditional spice in Japan for centuries. Gomasio should never be hot and should be added to dishes just before eating to preserve its nutty aroma. Gomasio is available in health food stores and Asian groceries. Gomasio should be stored in the refrigerator and consumed as soon as possible.

IN THE KITCHEN

AROMA:
Sesame does not smell and its taste is nutty and slightly sweet.

USE:
Sesame is used mainly as an ingredient in bread and rolls, muesli and in roast flakes in Central Europe. In Asian cuisine, meat and fish are fried in crunchy sesame butter, vegetable dishes are seasoned with gomasio, soups are spiced with tahini and sesame is added to sweet dishes of all types. Particularly in Chinese cuisine, sesame oil from roasted sesame seeds is often used as a spice.

BUYING/STORING:
Sesame is available in well-supplied supermarkets or in Turkish groceries. Buy sesame in whole seed form and store it in a cool, dark, dry place.

TIPS FOR COOKING:
Sesame develops its full nutty aroma only when roasted. For piquant dishes, crush the seeds in a mortar with a little salt to intensify the taste.
Sesame can go stale fast if it becomes damp.

Sinapis alba
Mustard

Origin:

Europe

Edible part:

Application:

FAMILY: Mustard (*Brassicaceae*)

SYNONYMS: White mustard

FORMS OF USE: Fruit (fresh and dried - crushed and ground)

ORIGIN: The mustard plant is native to the Mediterranean region. It is cultivated across Europe, particularly in France and Germany and has recently spread to North America, India and China.

PROPERTIES: Mustard grains grow on a 3 feet tall annual plant. The mustard plant resembles rabe both have similar yellow blooms and similarly shaped, green leaves. The yellow blooms change into pods containing mustard grains. Shortly before the mustard grains become ripe, the plants are reaped and dried. The grains are threshed and dried for the second time. The enzyme split when the mustard plant cells are eroded release substances causing the piquancy of mustard.

RELATED SPECIES: White mustard is related to black mustard (Brassica nigra), known as green or Dutch mustard, and brown mustard (Brassica juncea), or sarepta mustard. The black mustard is used exclusively as mustard, while the brown mustard is available in grain form as well. It is used in the same way as white mustard in cooking.

MYTHOLOGY: In the Bible, Jesus calls mustard a symbol of God's Kingdom. The Greeks and Romans used ground mustard as a spice and medical plant. According to Pliny, the Romans used mustard in about 40 different drugs. Dioscorides recommended it for epilepsy, spleen and liver pain.

MEDICINAL USE: Culpeper, an English doctor, prescribed mustard for a number of diseases from digestion problems to colds to toothaches and arthralgia, skin diseases and stiff necks. Crushed mustard corn mixed with water can be used as a compress when intensive promotion of blood circulation in skin is required in cases of lumbago, bronchitis or pleurisy.

DID YOU KNOW ...?

The English preferred freshly ground mustard corns, known as mustard flour, mixed with water and little vinegar. The renowned and traditional "Colman's Mustard," founded in 1814, is the mustard supplier for the Royal Court even today and is available in every good spice store. Mustard develops its typical sharpness only in contact with water because mustard oil, which causes the sharp taste, is released only in water. Heat prevents these processes and heated mustard has a milder taste.

PICKLING SPICE

Pickling spice is a mix of mustard corns, dill seeds, pepper, bay leaf and paprika. It is called "gherkin spice" or "marinade spice." Add cloves, ginger, chili or nutmeg for extra flavor as well. The taste of pickling spice is sweet and slightly sour and is ideal for pickles, pumpkins and other vegetables.

IN THE KITCHEN

AROMA:
Dried seeds do not smell, but their taste is sharp when chewed.

USE:
Mustard corn is used to season smoked meat, game and fish marinades. Mustard corns enhance the taste of vinegar gherkins, mixed pickles, aspics and cabbage dishes as well as green herrings and roast sirloin. Mustard powder goes well with poultry and beef. It gives a sweet and sour flavor to soups, sauces and pickled gherkins.

BUYING/STORING:
Mustard corns are available in well-supplied supermarkets or in spice stores. Mustard corns and powder can last for years if stored in a cool, dark place.

TIPS FOR COOKING:
We can recognize quality mustard when its corns are uniformly sized and it is golden in color.
Mustard flour is sharpest when mixed with water. Roast the powder or the corns with onions to flavor meats such as liver.

Symphytum officinale
Comfrey

Origin:

Europe

Edible part:

Use:

Property:

!

FAMILY: Borage (*Boraginaceae*)

SYNONYMS: Boneset, common comfrey

FORMS OF USE: Leaves and herbaceous stems (fresh, root, dried and ground)

ORIGIN: Comfrey is native to the temperate zones of Europe, western Asia and Asia Minor. In Central Europe, comfrey grows in wet places, meadow borders and along river banks.

PROPERTIES: Comfrey is a perennial and grows up to 3 feet high from a root in the shape of a beet. The plant is bristly pilous. Alternate leaves are lanceolate, up to 8 inches long and 1 inches wide. Its pilous leaves are dark green above and light green underneath. Hanging violet, bell-shaped blossoms form racemose inflorescence. The leaves contain allantoine.

RELATED SPECIES: Besides common European comfrey, Quaker comfrey (*Symphytum peregrinum*), originally native to Canada, is cultivated in Central Europe.

MEDICINAL USE: The leaves or ground roots of comfrey are used in alternative medicine even today to treat wounds including contusions, hematomas, vein pains, sprains, acne and rheumatism. It is said to be a successful cure for malignant tumors. Do not regularly drink tea prepared from the leaves because there is a suspicion that comfrey is carcinogenic. In the Middle Ages, comfrey was prescribed for bone fractures because allantoine promotes the growth of bone, cartilage and muscle cells.

DID YOU KNOW …?

The genus name "Symphytum" is derived from Greek "*symphyein*," or 'uniting,' which affirms the fact that the plant was highly appreciated for healing fractures during ancient times.

HAVE YOU EVER TASTED IT?

COMFREY POTATO SOUP
Wash and slice 1 leek. Wash, dry and cut 5 oz comfrey leaves. Wash and peel 1 lb potatoes and cut in ¾ in (1 cm) cubes. Melt about 1 ¾ tablespoons of butter in a pot and fry the leek, comfrey and potatoes. Add 3 cups broth and simmer for about 20 minutes. Season with salt, pepper and nutmeg.

IN THE KITCHEN

AROMA:
The taste of comfrey is fresh and spicy. Comfrey has no pronounced smell.

USE:
Comfrey should be consumed only in small quantities. Some people consume it plain like spinach. It goes well with salads and soups. A few generations ago, comfrey was an ingredient in pancakes.

IMPORTANT WARNING:

New studies suggest that consuming the plant in high quantities can cause liver cancer.

BUYING/STORING:
Comfrey is available in pharmacies. From a culinary perspective, dried comfrey is less interesting but more convenient than fresh comfrey. It can be kept in a bag in the vegetable compartment of the refridgerator only for a few days.

TIPS FOR COOKING:
Cut comfrey and freeze it with little water in the form of ice cubes.
Comfrey tolerates heat. Therefore, add it early to soup and cook.

Syzygium aromaticum
Cloves

Origin:

Asia

Edible part:

Use:

FAMILY: Myrtle (*Myrtaceae*)

SYNONYMS: Eugenia caryophyllatum, syzygium aromaticum

FORMS OF USE: Blossom buds (dried - whole or ground)

ORIGIN: Cloves are native to Indonesian Moluccas, the "Spice Islands." Today, the tree is grown in Indonesia, Madagascar, Tanzania, Sri Lanka and Malaysia.

PROPERTIES: The clove tree prospers best in tropical marine climates. It can grow up to 50 feet high and bear about 6 pounds of fruit per year from its sixth to its sixtieth year. It has and red blossoms narrow, cylindrical, evergreen leaves similar to bay leaves. As soon as the firmly closed green buds turn light red, they are picked manually, separated from the stems and dried in the sun. In this way, cloves turn the brown color by which we identify them. They are rich in essential oils.

MEDICINAL USE: Cloves promote digestion, relieve stomachaches, stimulate appetite, relieve pain and disinfect.

They heal toothaches as well. Clove oil is used as an anesthetic in dental surgery and as an ingredient in tooth fillings. Clove oil is sometimes administered for diarrhea and flatulence.

DID YOU KNOW …?
Half a lemon stuck with cloves helps to repel mosquitoes on warm, sultry days.

QUATRE ÉPICES

Quatre épices is a popular spice mix in France composed of cloves, black or white pepper, nutmeg and ginger. The name of the mix means "Four Spices," but it often contains other spices like paprika and cinnamon as well.

HAVE YOU EVER TASTED IT?

RUM GLÖGG
Heat 1 quart red wine, and add to 1 ½ cups port wine, the peel of 1 chemically untreated lemon, 8 cloves, 1 stick of cinnamon and 6 tablespoons sugar until it almost boils. Cover and steep for about 15 minutes. Take out the spice and lemon peel and add 1 cup warmed rum to the punch. Serve hot.

TIPS FOR COOKING
Do a "swimming test" with cloves: If their quality is good, they float with head up and herbaceous stem down on the surface of the water. If they float in a horizontal position on the water surface, their quality is poor.
When cooking cloves, it is good to stick them into an onion so that they can be more easily removed from a dish.
Cloves are a spice used best in pinches! If you use ground cloves, measure them carefully. Cloves go well with other strong spices like ginger, pepper or cardamom.

IN THE KITCHEN

AROMA:
The taste of cloves is fiery sharp and slightly hot. Cloves smell very strong.

USE:
Cloves enhance the taste of sweet dishes, baked goods and punch. They lend a special, piquant aroma to meat and fish dishes as well as game, poultry, stews, red cabbage, marinades of any type and smoked goods. Fine chocolates are delicious thanks to cloves, cinnamon and cardamom. Cloves are contained in various spice mixes such as Indian "garam masala," Arab "Baharat" and Chinese five-spice mix. Cloves are also present in Worchestershire sauce.

BUYING/STORING:
Whole cloves are preferred to powdered cloves because the essential oil evaporates very fast after cloves are ground. A spice grinder can grind a few cloves easily. Freshly ground cloves are perfect for Christmas cookies. Powdered and whole cloves can be kept in an airtight, dry and dark container for 2 – 3 years.

Tamarindus indica
Tamarind

Origin:

Africa

Edible part:

Use:
✕ ♣

FAMILY: Caesalpiniaceae

SYNONYMS: Tamarindo, magyi, imli

FORMS OF USE: Fruit flesh of siliquas, as paste or in a block

ORIGIN: The tamarind tree is native to Ethiopia and spread to India. It was brought to the Mediterranean region and to Central America in the 16th century. Today, it is cultivated worldwide, though not in great quantities.

PROPERTIES: Tamarinds are 2 – 8 inches long, cinnamon-colored brown siliquas, which are as wide as a finger and slightly coiled. The siliquas hang on an evergreen tree up to 82 feet high with very pinnate, oval-shaped leaves. They have beautiful blossoms, white outer petals and crimson-veined inner leaves with yellow edges. These blossoms develop into siliquas. Brownish black flesh tinged with red and ½ inch pits are covered with a fragile shell. The pits are removed and the flesh is dried and available as a block or paste. The taste is caused by a high content of fruit acids. Tamarind is rich

in tartaric acid and contains malic, succinic, citric and oxalic acids.

RELATED SPECIES: Tamarinds are divided by taste into two groups. Sweet tamarind has brownish, mushy, sweet fruit flesh and rounder seeds. Sour tamarind has slightly flat seeds, almost black flesh and sweet and sour taste reminiscent of sour candies.

MEDICINAL USE: Tamarind has laxative effects. In centuries past, the amount of vitamin C in tamarind was sufficient to protect sailors from scurvy.

DID YOU KNOW ...?

The Arabic word *"tamr hindi"* means "Indian dates."
Tamarind was probably exported in great amounts by India
and the seeds slightly resemble dates.

Others: In the Caribbean, refreshing lemonade is produced
of tamarind flesh, sugar and water. It is an exotic alternative to soda on hot summer days.

TIPS FOR COOKING

**Tamarind blocks must be dissolved in hot water. If a block still contains
seeds, they must be removed. If properly closed, you can keep the syrup
in the refridgerator for about a week.**

**Tofu is often pickled in tamarind syrup, which gives this neutral soy
product a pleasant flavor.**

The sour and fruity taste of tamarind goes well with sharp chili.

IN THE KITCHEN

AROMA:
Tamarind is pleasantly fruity and slightly sour.

USE:
Tamarind is a popular spice in East African, Indian, Asian and Latin American cuisines. It is used similarly to lemon juice or vinegar and is added to meat and fish dishes as well as to vegetables, rice and legume stews. Since tamarind is rich in pectin, it is used to thicken chutney, relish, jelly and marmalade. A popular south Indian specialty is *vindaalu*, a pork dish, probably derived from the Portuguese, *Porco vinho e alho*. In European cuisine, the popular Worcestershire sauce contains tamarind.

BUYING/STORING:
Tamarind siliquas, flesh, paste or syrup are available in spice stores or in stores selling Indian, Asian, Mexican or African specialties. Tamarind siliquas can be stored for months. When the siliquas are fragile, the fruit is older. However, the taste is still good. Paste is available in jars and is storable in blocks and as syrup for a long time.

Thymus vulgaris
Thyme

FAMILY: Mint (*Lamiaceae*)

SYNONYMS: Common thyme, garden thyme, frigoule

FORMS OF USE: Leaves (fresh and dried)

ORIGIN: Thyme is native to and is cultivated all over the Mediterranean region. Its aroma and flavor are heightened by sun exposure.

PROPERTIES: Thyme is a perennial evergreen forb whose lower herbaceous stems are woody or feathered. It grows up to about 16 inches high and has relatively small, dark green or grayish leaves. Its pink or lilac blossom is not very big. The whole plant has a very aromatic smell. The aroma of thyme is affected by essential oils, particularly thymol and carvacrol as well as flavonoid and tannin.

RELATED SPECIES: Lemon thyme (*Thymus citriodorus*) is a relative of garden thyme and is often used in cooking. Its leaves are slightly bigger and have yellow edges. It has a lemony scent, but its taste is reminiscent of thyme. It is

available in marketplaces in summer. Season desserts and fruit salads with it.

MYTHOLOGY: The word "Thymus" is derived from Greek "*thymos,*" or 'stamina' which symbolizes strength and power. The Greeks used thyme as a smoking plant. Roman legionaries took thyme baths before battle to give them courage and power.

MEDICINAL USE: In folk medicine, thyme is recommended as a cure for upper respiratory diseases. It releases cramps and mucus. Furthermore, it is believed to reduce fever, calm nerves, reduce odor and disinfect. It relieves asthma, digestion problems and sore throats.

HERBES DE PROVENCE

"Herbs of Provence," a French spice mix, comes from the French region of Provence and consists of indigenous herbs like thyme, rosemary, savory, oregano and lavender. A particular mix can include crushed bay leaf, fennel and a little grated orange peel as well. Strong spicy-piquant aroma is typical of this spice mix, which harmonizes very well with the simple rural food of the region. The mix always consists of dried herbs, which should be cooked for a longer time in order to bring out their aroma and flavor fully. Herbes de Provence goes well with meat, fruit and vegetable dishes.

HAVE YOU EVER TASTED IT?

HERB STUFFING

Peel and mince onion and 2 garlic cloves. Fry in 1 oz butter. Remove the crust from 2 slices of toast bread. Cut into small cubes. Tear off the leaves from 12 thyme twigs, mince and put into the pan with the bread cubes. Add 6 tablespoons sweet cream and simmer. Season with one tablespoon sherry, salt and pepper. Cut a pocket in a pork or lamb steak, fill in the mixture and roast in the oven at 400°F.

IN THE KITCHEN

AROMA:
The taste of thyme is spicy and distinctly resin-like. It has a strong smell.

USE:
Thyme goes well with meat and cabbage dishes, fish terrines, aromatic, fruity soups and sauces as well as with salads. Zucchini, pumpkins and tomatoes are often spiced with thyme.

BUYING/STORING:
Thyme is available either dried or fresh in supermarkets. Fresh thyme should be wrapped in a moist towel and put into a bag. It can be kept in the vegetable compartment of the refridgerator for about 1 week. The aroma of dried thyme is very intense. It should be stored in an airtight, closed container in a dark, cool place.

TIPS FOR COOKING:
Small quantities of thyme are sufficient and can be cooked for a longer time as well. Remove dried leaves from twigs with a fork. Thyme goes well with rosemary, oregano, sage and catmint.

Trachyspermum ammi
Ajowan

Origin:

Asia

Edible part:

Use:
✕ ♫

FAMILY: Carrot (Apiaceae)

SYNONYMS: Bistore's weed, ajonan, javanee

FORMS OF USE: Seeds (dried - whole and ground)

ORIGIN: This member of the carrot family is native to southern India. Today, the plant is grown in Central Asia, North Africa and Ethiopia. The seeds were used as a natural antiseptic in the ancient Orient.

PROPERTIES: An annual, herblike plant about 12 – 24 inches high with an umbel consisting of 5 to 15 small, white blossoms. The blossoms develop into dark brown pilous fruits about 1 mm wide and 4 mm long. The color and shape of the dried fruits resemble those of wild celery seeds.

RELATED SPECIES: Botanically, the ajowan plant is closely related to caraway and cumin.

IN THE KITCHEN

AROMA:
Ajowan tastes and smells like thyme. Its aftertaste is slightly sharp and bitter.

USE:
A classic spice of Indian and Arab cuisines, Ajowan is a necessary ingredient in dahls (legume dishes) and pankorhas (deep fried, savory bread prepared from egg dough), both because of its taste and because it promotes digestion. Furthermore, the spice goes well with pickles, root vegetables and grilled poultry dishes. It is essential in pilaf and is often an ingredient in curry mixes.

BUYING/STORING:
Ajowan is available in Arab and Indian groceries.
If stored in an airtight container in a cool, dark place, its whole seeds will last almost forever. If ground, the spice loses its pungent aroma and flavor.

TIPS FOR COOKING:
The taste of ajowan is very intense. Use it sparingly. The aroma and flavor are intensified with roasting.

Trigonella foenum-graecum
Fenugreek

Origin:

Asia

Edible part:

Use:

FAMILY: Legume (*Fabaceae*)

SYNONYMS: Greek clover, senegre, Alholva, hilbah, methi

FORMS OF USE: Leaves, fresh and dried, seeds, dried, whole or ground

ORIGIN: Fenugreek is native to Mesopotamia and was grown in the Mediterranean region in ancient times. Today, it is cultivated mainly in the Mediterranean as well as in central Asia.

PROPERTIES: Fenugreek grows up to 20 inches high and has strong roots. It blooms in June and July and has oval, light green leaves and yellowish-white blossoms. Fruit legumes containing seeds are characteristic.

RELATED SPECIES: Fenugreek is closely related to sweet trefoil (Trigonella caerulea), which is spread across the Alpine region. Baked potatoes are seasoned with the leaves of blue fenugreek and it is added to Schabziger (a Swiss cheese specialty originally from the Glarus canton).

MYTHOLOGY: In ancient Greece, fenugreek seeds roasted in barley oil were chewed by philosophers and their disciples to "encourage thinking." Today, it is known that fenugreek can improve athletic performance because the herb is rich in copper and iron and promotes the formation of red blood cells, supplying the cells with acids and nutrients.

MEDICINAL USE: Fenugreek is an ancient medicinal herb mentioned by Hippocrates. Fenugreek contains saponin and cumarine, which stabilize veins. Fenugreek can help to heal vascular diseases, varicose veins and hemorrhoids in particular. Furthermore, fenugreek has anti-inflammatory properties and, therefore, natural medicine prescribes it for rheumatism and gall bladder diseases. Fenugreek promotes bile flow and lowers cholesterol.

Did you know ...?
Its botanical name "Trigonella" is probably derived from its triangle blossoms. *Foenum graecum* is derived from Latin and means "Greek hay."

Have you ever tasted it?

Indian potato soup
Peel, wash and cube 1 lb potatoes. Clean, peel and slice 2 carrots. Fry potatoes and carrot in a pot briefly with 1 oz melted butter. Sprinkle with salt, 1 teaspoon curry and 1 teaspoon ground fenugreek. Baste with 3 cups broth and cook in a closed pot on medium heat for about 15 minutes. Clean and slice ½ bundle green onion. Make a partial purée of the potato soup, serve on plates and garnish with green onion.

IN THE KITCHEN

AROMA:
The taste of fenugreek is spicy, bitter and slightly floury. Its smell slightly resembles freshly milled hay.

USE:
Fenugreek is used mainly in India and in the Arab states of Africa. It is indispensable for seasoning Indian curry and chutney dishes and it improves Egyptian and Ethiopian stews and fish, meat and vegetable dishes. Its seeds are used to spice bread and small Arab pastries.

BUYING/STORING:
Fenugreek is available in seed and ground form in Indian groceries or spice stores. Keep fenugreek in an airtight, container in a cool, dark place. Ground fenugreek should be bought only in the smallest possible quantities and quickly consumed because it quickly loses its aroma.

TIPS FOR COOKING:
Before crushing, roast the seeds slightly. At too high temperatures, the seeds turn red and bitter. The seeds do not taste good if unripe and they must always be cooked with other ingredients.

Vanilla planifolia
Vanilla

Origin:

America

Edible part:

Use:

FAMILY: Orchid (*Orchidaceae*)

SYNONYMS: Vanilla orchid, vanille

FORMS OF USE: Fruit pods or seeds, dried

ORIGIN: This climbing orchid, is native to southern Mexico, Guatemala and other Central American countries. Today, vanilla is grown both in Central America and on Madagascar and the Reunion and Comoros islands. High quality vanilla is called "bourbon vanilla."

PROPERTIES: Vanilla beans are the long, thin fruits of the vanilla orchid, which climbs 50 feet high tropical trees. The plant has thick, fleshy, oval leaves 10 inches long and 3 inches wide. The blossom is relatively small compared to the leaves and its color is white-yellow or greenish. Wild blossoms open only for a few hours and are pollinated by hummingbirds. Vanilla in cultivated form is pollinated manually. In 6 – 8 months, the vanilla stripes are harvested unripe and then fermented. The green-yellow fruits turn black-brown and develop an intense aroma. Vanillin is the most aromatic substance of this spice.

MYTHOLOGY: The Aztecs spiced their chocolate with vanilla to increase sexual desire. Indigenous peoples from North America used dried vanilla as currency.

MEDICINAL USE: The Indians used vanilla both as a spice and as a medicine. They attributed heart-stimulating effects to it. Like cacoa, vanilla is said to reduce fear, depression and fatigue.

Did you know …?

The difference between vanilla sugar and vanillin sugar is that vanilla sugar is produced from genuine vanilla. Vanillin sugar contains only synthetically produced vanillin, an aromatic substance which smells like vanilla.

You can make vanilla sugar yourself: Put 1 scraped-out pod with 1 cup sugar in a jar with a lid and set aside for at least 6 weeks.

Have you ever tasted it?

Homemade vanilla ice cream

Heat 1 cup milk and 7 tablespoons sweet cream. Cut the vanilla bean in half lengthwise, scrape out its flesh and put the bean and 1 pinch of salt in the milk. Boil and stir. Cool. Whip 3 yolks and 6 tablespoons sugar in a warm water bath to make cream. Add milk mixture to the yolks slowly. Blend everything until thick. Cool and refrigerate for about an hour. Whip 1 cup sweet cream until thick and add to the chilled ice cream. Put everything in an ice cream maker and freeze for 15-20 minutes. If you do not have an ice cream maker, put the ice cream in a container and blend for 5 minutes. When the ice cream thickens, freeze 3-6 hours.

In the kitchen

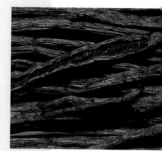

AROMA:
The smell of vanilla is intense and slightly sweet. Its taste is also sweet and slightly spicy.

USE:
Vanilla is used to season chocolate, coffee, desserts of any type, custard, stewed fruit, and fruit salads. The taste of battercakes, pastries and cakes is improved with vanilla. In Mexico, even savory food like shellfish and meat dishes are seasoned with vanilla.

BUYING/STORING:
Vanilla is among the most expensive spices. You can buy vanilla beans in jars in every well-supplied supermarket. Excellent quality vanilla is available under the name "bourbon-vanilla." When buying vanilla beans in a spice store, you can choose between various qualities and origins. Vanilla beans should be stored in an airtight, container in a cool, dark place.

TIPS FOR COOKING:
In order to use the flesh, cut the fruit lengthwise and scrape it out. The fruit is not edible on its own.

Wasabia japonica
Wasabi

FAMILY: Mustard (*Brassicaceae*)

SYNONYMS: Green horseradish

FORMS OF USE: Herbaceous stem, dried and ground

ORIGIN: Wasabi is native to Japan, but is also cultivated in other Asian countries as well as New Zealand and Australia.

PROPERTIES: Wasabi prospers in both wet soil and shallow water. The shape of its leaves resembles Indian cress and its thickness resembles cabbage leaves. Dried wasabi powder comes from the thick lower part it the woody stem.

MEDICINAL USE: Wasabi plays an important role in Japanese medicine. Recent studies prove that wasabi contains a substance that dilutes blood and has a positive effect on stomach cancer.

IN THE KITCHEN

AROMA:
The taste of wasabi and its powder resemble sharp horseradish.

USE:
Wasabi is an important spice in Japanese cuisine. Sushi and sashimi (raw fish) are usually seasoned with wasabi. It also goes well with boiled meat and fish.

BUYING/STORING:
Fresh wasabi is hard to find. However, the powder is always available in Asian stores. Tightly sealed and kept in a dark, dry place, wasabi will last for years. It loses its aroma very slowly.

TIPS FOR COOKING:
In order to make paste from wasabi powder, mix with water at a proportion of 1:1.
The paste can be stored in a clean, covered jar for several days in the refridgerator.

Zanthoxylum piperitum
Sezchuan pepper

Origin:

Asia

Edible part:

Use:

Property:

!

FAMILY: Rue (*Rutaceae*)

SYNONYMS: -

FORMS OF USE: Fruits, dried, whole and ground

ORIGIN: The Zanthoxylum genus is grown all over Asia. Some species grow on the American and African continents as well. Sezchuan pepper exported to Europe is grown mainly in southern China and Vietnam.

PROPERTIES: Sezchuan pepper corns are the dried fruits from a relatively small tree with pinnate leaves and white or greenish blossoms. The fruit is harvested unripe and dried. The fruits contain essential oils, mainly terpene, geraniol, linalool, cineole, and citronellal. Its spicy taste is caused by amid, which is contained mainly in the fruit walls. Its seeds are bitter and should be removed.

RELATED SPECIES: Zanthoxylum rhetsa grows in northern India and sansho pepper grows in Japan.

MEDICINAL USE: Sezchuan pepper is rich in essential oils which stimulate salivation and digestion.

IMPORTANT WARNING:

In large quantities, Sezchuan pepper dulls the taste buds and can irritate the stomach.

SICHIMI TOGARASHI

Sichimi togarashi is a Japanese seven-spice mix consisting of Sezchuan pepper, chili, dried orange peel, poppy seeds, black sesame, tamarind and seaweed crushed in a mortar. The mix is fiery sharp and the Japanese use it as a table spice. This mix is available in Asian speciality stores. Use it sparingly.

HAVE YOU EVER TASTED IT?

SUKIYAKI
Have 2 lb sirloin cut into thin slices by a butcher. Wash and chop 12 fresh shiitake mushrooms, 6 green onions, ½ chinese cabbage, 1 handful spinach, 2 leeks, 8 large mushrooms and 2 carrots. Place on big plates according to shape and color. Heat a little margarine in a hot wok, greasing the bottom and the walls well. Add 1 tablespoon sugar and ½ teaspoon Sezchuan pepper, caramelize the sugar. Before it is too dark, add a little saké, soy sauce and water. Gradually add 2 tablespoons sugar, up to ½ put saké, ½ put soy sauce and 1 cup water in order to prepare a concentrated bouillon. It should be about 1 inch high in the pot. Boil vegetable and meat in the bouillon. Season the meat with the mix prepared from sechuan pepper and salt.

IN THE KITCHEN

AROMA:
Sezchuan pepper has a peppery, fresh taste slightly similar to lemon.

USE:
Sezchuan pepper is a classic spice in Asian cuisine. It goes well with fish as well as with pork, chicken and duck. Noodle and rice soups are dusted with it and it is essential in Japanese Sukiyaki-Grills.

BUYING/STORING:
Sezchuan pepper is available in well-supplied supermarkets, spice shops or Asian specialty stores. It is available either whole or ground. Whole fruit pods are preferable to powder because they keep their aroma longer. Sezchuan pepper should be stored in an air-tight container at a cool, dark place.

TIPS FOR COOKING:
Sezchuan pepper is roasted without any fat in order to develop its aroma fully. It is then crushed in a mortar.
Do not cook Sezchuan pepper too long because it loses its taste fast. Dishes are usually seasoned shortly before being served.

Zingiber officinale
Ginger

Origin:

Asia

Edible part:

Use:

FAMILY: Ginger (*Zingiberaceae*)

SYNONYMS: Canton ginger, zingiber officinale, stem ginger, gingembre, gengibre

FORMS OF USE: Root, fresh, dried, ground into powder or pickled

ORIGIN: The ginger plant is a perennial grown in the tropics. It is probably native to southern and central Asia. The plant is cultivated in India, Indonesia, China, Japan, Australia, South America and Nigeria.

PROPERTIES: Ginger is a reedy plant sometimes more than 3 feet high. It has narrow leaves and buds from which individual yellow-red blossoms develop. It contains essential oils and resin (galangol, alpinol), which cause its distinctive taste. More precisely, it is the rhizome, known as "ginger root" although it is not a root botanically speaking, which gives ginger its taste.

MYTHOLOGY: In 500 BC, Confucius, a philosopher, seasoned dishes with ginger. Daily consumption of ginger was believed to guarantee long life.

MEDICINAL USE: Ginger tea and ginger baths are prescribed in Asian alternative medicine for rheumatism, muscle pain or colds. Ginger stimulates the appetite, promotes digestion and relieves stomach cramps.

TANDOORI

This Indian spice mix, sometimes called "adoori," consists of ginger, garlic, tamarind, cumin, turmeric, coriander seeds and Cayenne pepper. Some mixes contain chili powder, paprika, cinnamon or cloves as well. Tandoori is spicy and fruity and is used to season poultry and lamb.

HAVE YOU EVER TASTED IT?

KIWI CHUTNEY
Peel and cube 5 kiwis. Peel 4 shallots and peel a 2 inch long piece of ginger. Boil 2 tablespoons brown sugar and ½ cup water. Add the kiwi cubes and cook until soft. Add ginger, shallots, 3 tablespoons raisins, ½ teaspoon crushed coriander seeds, ½ grated lemon and its juice, 2 tablespoons mild vinegar and cook uncovered, stirring occasionally. Pour the chutney into jars and let cool.

IN THE KITCHEN

AROMA:
The taste of ginger is spicy, fruity and aromatic. It smells spicy and sharp.

USE:
Ginger is a common spice in Asian cuisines. However, it has been popular in England as well since the heyday of the British Empire, which stretched over much of Asia during the 19th century. Ginger is used to season curry dishes and stews, poultry and lamb as well as fish and seafood. Ground ginger enhances gingerbread, rice milk and fruit salads.

BUYING/STORING:
Fresh ginger is available in the produce section of well-supplied supermarkets. Ginger lasts for 2 – 3 weeks in the refridgerator. Ginger powder is found among the spices in most grocery stores. If closed in an airtight container in a cool, dark place, it will last for months. Pickled ginger is available in Asian specialty stores. Refridgerate after opening.

TIPS FOR COOKING:
Fresh ginger is peeled and then grated or cut into very thin slices. Use it with discretion: its spiciness differs depending on its age.

Chili sauces and pastes
American chili sauces

PRODUCTS: Tabasco and Caribbean chili sauces

TABASCO

HISTORY: Tabasco is native to Louisiana in the Deep South of the United States. Edmund McIlhenny, the inventor of the world-famous chili sauce, was a spice and sauce aficionado. He cultivated the first chili peppers in about 1860 and started experimenting with his harvest. His passion for hot dishes gave him the idea to preserve fresh chili peppers so that they lose as little piquancy as possible. McIlhenny discovered a method of grinding pepper pods and preserving them with salt. His friends could taste the result of his work – and were astonished. His business sense led him to sell his invention. He sold the sauce under the name Tabasco – a Native American Indian word meaning "country where soil is hot and moist."

MANUFACTURING METHOD: Tabasco is manufactured in the same way 130 years later. It is a pure and natural product. Chili peppers are harvested from September to December. The pepper pods are ground and mixed with a little salt on harvest day. The mixture is poured into oak casks and aged for 3 years. As it ferments, it develops its full spicy aroma.

When the chili pepper mix has rested longenough, unwanted liquid is drained and distilled vinegar is added. Everything is blended continuously for 4 weeks. Then the remaining shucks and seed corns are separated. The red sauce is bottled, packed in cardboard boxes and distributed all over the world.

The proportion of ingredients contained in the mix, namely chili peppers, salt and distilled vinegar, is not known because it is a fiercely guarded family secret.

TABASCO GREEN PEPPER SAUCE

A sister of the red pepper sauce was invented in 1996: Tabasco green pepper sauce. It is milder and is made from aromatic Jalapeno peppers. This sauce is intended for lovers of mildly hot dishes.

CARIBBEAN CHILI SAUCE

There are a number of Caribbean chili sauces. They have one thing in common - all of them contain cut chili, onion, vinegar and salt. Depending on the particular chili sauce, the color can be

TIPS FOR COOKING

Use chili sauces sparingly because some of them are extremely hot. Tabasco green pepper sauce is very mild and you can add a teaspoon of this variant to many dishes. American chili sauces are very popular. Fans of fiery, hot flavor might add more spice to their food even at the table.

bright red (if it contains tomatoes) or yellow (if it contains turmeric).

IN THE KITCHEN

AROMA:
Depending on the particular type, American chili sauces are extremely hot or sweet-sharp. Tabasco green pepper hot sauce is mild compared to Red Tabasco.

USE:
This fiery sauce gives powerful flavor to both salsa and stews like jambalaya and chili con carne. Chicken wings and burrito fillings, enchiladas and wraps are seasoned with a few drops of this sauce and every genuine, proud Southerner livens up his omelet, scrambled eggs or breakfast eggs with this extremely hot sauce.

BUYING/STORING:
Tabasco, as well as other Caribbean chili sauces, is available in every well-supplied supermarket.
Keep unopened chili sauces in the cupboard. Opened bottles stored in the refridgerator will keep for a long time.

Asian Chili Sauces

PRODUCTS: Chinese, Korean, Thai and Malaysian chili sauce, sambals, harissa

CHINESE AND KOREAN CHILI SAUCES

Besides soy sauce, chili sauce is the most important relish in Asia. It is usually very salty and is used as a kind of salt substitute in traditional Asian cuisine. In China, it is common mainly in the Sezchuan and Hunan provinces.

THAI AND MALAYSIAN CHILI SAUCES

These Asian chili sauces differ from Chinese and Korean varieties because they usually contain a good deal of ginger. Their consistency is thicker than that of other chili sauces.

SAMBALS

Sambals are pastes ro-
ther than sauces. They
are made from chili
peppers. You can still
spot little pieces of the
pods in the product.
They originated in Indo-
nesian cuisine, but are
now a fixture in the
cuisines of many other
Asian countries.

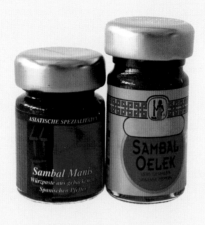

They come in various flavors. Sambal Oelek, sometimes called
Ulek, is the best-known chili paste. It is extremely hot and should
be added to dishes only in very small quantities. Sambal manis
is a sweet and rather mild paste. It is a mix of chili and shrimp,
enhanced with Kaffir lime leaves, Kemer (pistachio) nuts, brown
sugar and oil.

Most sambals are soft at room temperature, but some are solid
and sold in blocks. The most popular one is sambal kacang,
which includes ground peanuts. It must be diluted with hot
water before use.

AFRICAN CHILI PASTE

HARRISSA

This chili paste is from North Africa. It is extremely hot and is produced from dried or fresh chili. Harrissa also contains garlic, salt, cumin, coriander and mint. Milder versions contain tomato as well. It is used in Arab cuisine to season soups and stews and to color mayonnaise and rice. Lamb, chicken and fish are marinated in it before grilling. This hot paste is served with couscous in North Africa.

HAVE YOU EVER TASTED?

VEGETABLE SOUFFLÉ WITH MILLET CRUST
Simmer 7 tablespoons millet and more than ½ cup vegetable broth in a covered pot for about 30 minutes. Peel and half 4 carrots. Cut 4 small zuchini into narrow strips and clean 10 oz oyster mushrooms and cut in wide strips. Cook the mushrooms and vegetables. Peel and mince two shallots. Press one garlic clove in 2 tablespoons oil, then cook the shallots and garlic until glassy. Add the millet, 1 egg, 3½ tablespoons cream, 7 tablespoons grated parmesan, 2 tablespoons pumpkin seeds and onion-garlic mix. Season with salt, pepper and nutmeg. Put the vegetable in the soufflé dish and spread the millet mixture on top. Bake in a preheated oven for about 25 minutes at 392°F. Harrisa goes well with this dish.

HAVE YOU EVER TASTED IT?

GINGER CHICKEN AND CURRY RICE

Boil 1 cup water in a pot. Add salt, 1 teaspoon curry and ½ cup rice. Simmer everything for 15 - 20 minutes and add more warm water, if necessary. The water should evaporate completely, leaving behind cooked rice.

Clean 2 green onions, cut into narrow slices. Peel 1 little piece of fresh ginger root and grate finely. Clean and cut 1 red pepper into strips.

Heat 1 tablespoon sunflower oil in a big pan and stew the green onion. Sprinkle 2 chicken breast fillets with 1 tablespoon lemon juice, place in the pan and cook for about 1 minute quickly on each side. Add ginger, red pepper, ½ cup vegetable broth and 3 tablespoons of cocoa milk and simmer covered 5 - 10 minutes. Add 3½ oz bamboo shoots and season everything with ½ teaspoon salsa. Wash, dry and finely cut 1 bundle cilantro. Serve the chicken with the sauce and curry rice on two plates. Garnish with the chopped cilantro.

IN THE KITCHEN

AROMA:
Depending on the particular type, some Asian chili sauces taste hot and salty while others are pleasantly hot and fruity.

USE:
Chili sauces and sambals are used to season fish dishes, poultry dishes and cold sauces. They are both used in dishes prepared in a wok as well as in soups. Sambals both season rice and color it red.

BUYING/STORING:
Asian chili sauces and sambals are available in well-supplied supermarkets or Asian groceries.
If unopened, they can be stored for a long time without losing their aroma or flavor. Once opened, they will keep in the refridgerator for several months.

TIPS FOR COOKING:
Hot sambals and chili sauces can substitute for fresh or dried chili peppers in dishes.
Sambals, available in blocks, must be dissolved in a little hot water so that you can measure them better.

Curry and curry pastes
Curry

PRODUCTS: Madras, Ceylon, Vindaloo

HISTORY: Curry is the best-known spice mix. Although it is an Indian product, Englishmen invented it. British colonizers took a fancy to the aromatic cuisine of India. They wanted to enjoy its aromatic dishes both within the colonial area and at home on their cold island. When they learned how many different kinds of spices are used in Indian cooking, they thought it would be impossible to imitate such complicated dishes at home in England. However, they finally came up with the idea to make a universal spice to season all Indian dishes in England. The Englishmen named this mix "curry." In India, the term "curry" includes meat or fish dishes that are prepared in a spicy yellow sauce. Each Indian housewife mixes her own curry mix for each meal separately.

MANUFACTURING METHOD: Curry usually consists of ground spices. Most curry mixes consist of 10 to 20 or more spices. There is no standard formula. The yellow color of curry is caused by ground turmeric. The redder the curry, the higher its share of chili powder and the

hotter the flavor. The most important ingredients in curry are ginger, cardamom, cumin, pepper, coriander, allspice and fenugreek seeds. Cloves, cinnamon, mace, cayenne pepper and paprika are used often as well as other spices like dried coconut milk powder, lemon grass or curry leaf. Some curries include salt or vegetable flour.

Some curry mixes also include ingredients other than ground spices.

CURRY TYPES

Bengali curry powder: Curry powder from northeast India is extremely spicy compared to other mixes. The share of cumin, coriander and chili is slightly higher in this curry than in the other types.

Madras curry powder: Curry powder from the southeastern port of Madras and its surrounding regions is usually fruity and mild. It typically contains ground cardamom with green pods. Madras curry powder has a very full aroma.

Ceylon curry powder: This spice mix reflects the character of Sri Lanka. The taste of the curry is slightly salty like the sea and is hotter than the other types because of the pepper.

Vindaloo curry powder: This powder is native to Goa, controlled by Portugal until 1962. Because the powder contains a high amount of garlic and tamarind, Vindaloo curry powder is very mild and slightly sour.

IN THE KITCHEN

Aroma:
Depending on the type, the ingredients in curry are fruity, spicy or hot. Curry mixes often contain a description of their flavor on the package.

Use:
Curry and rice are usually inseparable. However, you can spice meat, fish and vegetable dishes with curry powder as well. It goes particularly well with okra, root vegetables and legumes as well as with bananas or mangoes.

Buying/storing:
You can buy curry powder in every good supermarket, but special, extraordinary curry mixes are only available in spice shops or Asian groceries. Keep curry in an airtight container in a cool, dark place if you plan to store it for a long time.

Tips for cooking:
Curry powder develops its full aroma when it is cooked in a little fat. Do not cook too long because it burns fast and becomes bitter. Have a little broth or water at hand to add if necessary.
Curry powder goes well mainly with coconut milk, chili, onion and garlic.

Curry pastes

PRODUCTS: Green, red massamam

HISTORY: Curry pastes do not, however, come exclusively from India. They are common in Indonesia and Thailand as well. Just as there are many types of curry powder, there are many varieties of curry pastes. The pastes differ in their ingredients and are available in various flavors and colors.

MANUFACTURING METHOD: Curry pastes are usually thick and good for spreading. They are generally roasted in fat, preserved in oil and contain red and green chili peppers. Other spices often found in curry paste include coriander, cumin, ginger and garlic. Shrimp paste, roasted peanuts and stewed onion are sometimes added as well. Depending on the individual flavor desired, a cook may supplement the paste with lemongrass, cinnamon, clove, Chinese anis or cardamom. In the West, curry pastes are poured into jars with screw-on lids.

TYPES OF CURRY PASTES

Red curry paste: This paste is very popular in Indonesia and consists of coriander, cumin, black pepper, shrimp paste, nutmeg, red chilies, oil, lemon grass, garlic, fresh coriander roots, green coriander, Kaffir lime leaves, salt and a little turmeric. Its red color is caused by the large number of chili peppers. Red curry paste is extremely hot and refreshing at the same time.

Green curry paste: Green curry paste is also very popular in Indonesia. Unlike red curry-paste, it contains green chili peppers, onion, fresh galangal and a lot of green coriander. Do not underestimate its spiciness!

Massamam curry paste: Massamam curry paste is a specialty from South Thailand prepared of dried chili peppers. It contains coriander, cumin, pepper, fresh galangal, shrimp paste, lemon grass, onion and garlic. The cloves balance its aroma and give the paste its distinctive taste.

Madras curry paste: An Indian curry paste consisting of chili, ginger, onion, garlic and coconut powder. Additionally, it is seasoned with cumin, coriander, cardamom, cinnamon, curry leaf and turmeric. Oil and vinegar bind this spice mix together.

HAVE YOU EVER TASTED IT?

HOMEMADE CURRY POWDER

Crush 5 green cardamom pods and remove the seeds. Roast in a pan without any fat with 6 tablespoons cumin, 2 tablespoons coriander seeds, 2 tablespoons fenugreek seeds and 4 little dried red chili peppers. Stir ingredients continuously for a few minutes. Then grind everything with a mortar or in a coffee grinder. Add 3 knife-pointfuls ground cloves, 3 knife-pointfuls ground nutmeg, 2 tablespoons cinnamon, 1 tablespoon ginger powder and 2 tablespoons turmeric powder. Keep the mix in a tightly closed container.

IN THE KITCHEN

AROMA:
Depending on the particular type, the taste of curry pastes is fiery or pleasantly hot and fruity.

USE:
Curry pastes are used to season fish, poultry and lamb dishes. They are mixed with vegetables and enhance the taste of rice dishes.

BUYING/STORING:
Curry pastes are available in Asian specialty stores, spice shops and in well-supplied supermarkets. If unopened, they can be stored forever. Once opened, keep in the refridgerator, particularly when ginger is one of the ingredients. They should keep for several months.

TIPS FOR COOKING:
Add curry pastes to dishes or use as a marinade for meat and fish. Be careful because they are usually extremely hot and usually have a powerful aftertaste.
Curry pastes dilute very well in warm dishes. They must be mixed very properly in cold dishes.

Fish sauces and pastes
Asian Products

Origin:

Asia, Europe

Edible part:
Everything

Use:
✗

PRODUCTS: Oyster sauce, Asian fish sauce, shrimp paste, anchovy paste, salmon paste, caviar crème

HISTORY: In the past, and today in poorer areas, no one ever threw away anything edible. Pastes were produced of the remains of fish, shellfish and shells.

MANUFACTURING METHOD: Regardless of whether it is fish or shrimp paste, the manufacturing method is the same. Boned fish or shellfish are cured with salt and fermented. Depending on the particular region, the basic ingredient is soy sauce and/or various spices. The result is usually similar: a salty paste, smelling intensely of fish, with a liquid, creamy or even crumbly consistency.
The names differ from country to country: "trassi" in Indonesia, "blachan" in Malaysia and "gapi" in Thailand.

SHRIMP PASTE

This extremely hot paste is made from dried shrimp meat and salt. It smells intensely like fish, but this smell disap-

pears when it is cooked. It is available in tins, jars or in blocks. It goes well with Indonesian meat and poultry dishes.

ASIAN FISH SAUCE

This sauce is prepared from fermented fish like mackerels, anchovies and cuttlefish. It contains a lot of salt and performs the same task in Thailand and Vietnam as a salt shaker on our tables. It is used instead of salt to season stir-fry dishes prepared in woks, or soups and sauces.

OYSTER SAUCE

This sauce is thick and dark with a liquid consistency. Its ingredients include boiled, fermented oyster meat and soy sauce. It is universally used in Southeast Asia to season fish, meat and vegetable dishes.

HAVE YOU EVER TASTED IT?

BEEF AND MUSHROOMS
Cut 9 oz shell steak in narrow stripes. Add 3 tablespoons Marsala, 3 tablespoons soy sauce, 1 tablespoon anchovy paste and 1 tablespoon starch. Pour over the meat and macerate for 30 minutes. Peel a small piece ginger and mince. Peel 1 garlic clove and 2 small onions and cut into fine slices. Clean and quarter 3½ oz mushrooms. Fry in hot oil, stirring constantly. Remove the beef from the marinade for 3 minutes. Add ginger, garlic and onion. Add the marinade and simmer for 3 minutes. Season with salt and pepper and sprinkle with roasted sesame seeds. Serve with rice.

IN THE KITCHEN

AROMA:
Depending on the type, Asian fish sauces and pastes are salty or hot.

USE:
Fish sauces and pastes are used to season fish and meat dishes, stir-frys prepared in the wok, and soups and sauces.

BUYING/STORING:
Fish sauces and pastes are available in Asian specialty stores in bottled liquid form, as spreadable pastes in jars, and as hard blocks. You can store them forever and they will not lose their aroma. You can store even opened packages in the refridgerator for years.

TIPS FOR COOKING:
Always add sauces and pastes to hot liquid. Make sure that the solid pastes are diluted.
Because the salt content in fish sauces and pastes is usually very high, additional salt is often not necessary.

European Products

CAVIAR CRÈME
A caviar crème does not necessarily contain solely sturgeon eggs. It can, and often does, contain codfish eggs. You can tell whether a paste contains genuine caviar by its price. Besides eggs, the crème contains oil, vinegar, salt, sugar and potato flakes. Depending on the particular type, spices like dill or mustard flour are also added. The crème is slightly salty and must be kept cold.

SALMON CRÈME
Salmon crème is a specialty from northern Europe consisting of salmon, codfish eggs, oil, vinegar and salt. It must be kept cool and cannot be stored for very long. It is delectable with hard-boiled eggs and is good for seasoning sauces, soups or spreads.

ANCHOVY PASTE
Anchovy paste is made from anchovy meat, salt and little vinegar. Depending on the particular variant, the paste can contain various spices as well. The Spanish, southern French and Italian claim this paste as one of their respective national or regional specialties, but it is available in tubes all over the world. You can enhance the taste of some sauces with it. It must be kept in a cold place and it is spreadable.

IN THE KITCHEN

AROMA:
European fish sauces and pastes contain mostly fish and are slightly salty.

USE:
Fish sauces and pastes are used to season sauces and soups. In particular, they intensify the taste of fish dishes. They go well with hard-boiled eggs and can be spread on bread.

BUYING/STORING:
Anchovy crème is available in a tube in almost any supermarket. If you want to buy caviar or salmon crème, it is advisable to visit a delicatessen. Fish pastes and crèmes cannot be stored for a long time and should be kept in the fridge. They must be consumed quickly once opened.

TIPS FOR COOKING:
European fish pastes – except anchovy crème – do not tolerate any heat and can only be added to dishes cold or shortly before a dish is served.

The quality of anchovy crème is reflected in the price of the product.

Salty extracts

Origin:

Europe

Edible part:
Everything

Use:
✗

PRODUCTS: Bouillon cubes, granulated broth, yeast extract

BOUILLON CUBES/ GRANULATED BROTH

HISTORY: Bouillon cubes are classic soup spices. Sold by the Maggi company for the first time in 1900, they have been an integral part of its assortment ever since. Bouillon cubes became the basis of soups and stews in the 1970's and 1980's, but lately they have been replaced by granulated broth or instant broth. Frequently substituted for salt, bouillon cubes remain essential ingredients in broths.

MANUFACTURING METHOD: Bouillon cubes consist of thickened meat or vegetable extract. The water is drained and the extract is freeze-dried in cubes. Bones, meat, and cubed vegetable are roasted in fat and placed in water to simmer. The individual ingredients slowly release substances while simmering. All is seasoned with spices and salt. If industrially prepared, this broth is thickened and freeze-dried.

Yeast extract

HISTORY: In the 19th century, Justus von Liebig, a German chemist, and Louis Pasteur, a French biologist and chemist, invented a procedure to produce industrial extracts which could last a long time. Yeast extract as a spice experienced its renaissance at the beginning of the last century along with the discovery of vitamin B and its effect on human organisms because yeast is rich in B-vitamin.

MANUFACTURING METHOD: There are two methods for manufacturing yeast extract. In autolysis, 122° F (50°C) warm water is added to yeast cultures. At this temperature, yeast cells die, but the enzymes of cell contents remain active. The yeast enzymes erode the cell walls and the contents can leave while the proteins decompose into amino acids. The liquid is consequently filtered and evaporated. Acid hydrolysis is a chemical process in which yeast cultures are heated and neutralized with hydrochloride acids, caustic soda or with sodium carbonate. The decomposition and fermentation of yeast cultures are accelerated in the second process.

HAVE YOU ALREADY TASTE IT?

HOT TOMATO SOUP
Chop 1 red onion, crush 2 large, canned tomatoes and preserve their juice. Heat 2 tablespoons oil in a pot and fry the onion, 1 pressed garlic, and the tomatoes and juice. Season with ½ teaspoon oregano and ½ teaspoon chili powder, a pinch salt, 1 teaspoon granulated broth and 1 tablespoon sugar. Simmer for 10 minutes.
Serve with diced avocado shrimps and croutons.

In the kitchen

Aroma:
All salty extracts are, obviously, salty. They tend also to be spicy and piquant.

Use:
Salty extracts are popular products and substitute for salt in piquant dishes. Besides seasoning soups and stews, they are used to spice meat and fish dishes, vegetable dishes, sauces, soufflés and savory cakes.

Buying/storing:
Their best-before data is always printed on the package. The products should be stored in a dry, dark and cool place, such as a cupboard. The jars should be closed very tightly because the extracts absorb humidity from the air, which makes measuring the instant powder more difficult.

Tips for cooking:
Use salty extracts instead of salt, but watch out! Too much salt is overpowering.

Many instant powders are added to cold dishes while others only to hot liquids. When preparing a cold dish, pay attention to the directions on the package.

Mustard

PRODUCTS:

DEPENDING ON FLAVOR: sweet, mild, medium hot, hot, extra hot mustard

DEPENDING ON ORIGIN: German, French, English, American mustard

HISTORY: Mustard is among the oldest spice pastes in the world. In ancient Egypt, Greece and Rome, mustard flour was considered a spice and was used to preserve meat. A recipe from the 4th century written by a Roman named Paladius proves that mustard with the same composition as today existed in ancient times: honey, olive oil, vinegar and ground mustard seeds.

Mustard definitely existed in the Rhine area during Roman times, but it became truly popular in Germany and France around the 10th century. In the British Isles, mustard was discovered only in the 12th century. In 1634, the city of Dijon was granted the sole right to produce mustard in France and it is still famous all over Europe as a mustard-producing town.

Mashbottich in the mustard mill in Monschau.

Since mustard grows everywhere in temperate climates, there are regional mustard varieties all over Europe. Some places have a very long tradition of producing mustard, others have disappeared with globalization and a few are currently experiencing a revival. Mustards can be found in all European countries. Whether made in the Czech Republic, Sweden or Belgium, specialties are everywhere. Based on the fact that the most commonly known and exported types are German, French and English, only these mustards will be discussed in detail, which, however, should not be regarded as the devaluation of other national mustards.

Manufacturing method: Mustard corns are crushed and the seeds are poured into a break roll, with the shells peeling off in the process. Industrially produced mustard types made in bulk are pressed at high pressure. Then mustard oil is partially squeezed and the mustard cake is ground into fine powder in dry flour runs. In little mustard mills, the mustard groat is mixed with vinegar and salt in a Mashbottich. The mustard mash rests in order to develop its special individual flavor before it is ground. The mustard gets its special consistency during the intensive binding of all ingredients. Mustard flour can contain, depending on its degree of milling, 3 to 4 times more water. The procedure is caused by the swelling capacity of carbohydrates. In traditional production, aroma develops better and essential oils are preserved in higher quantities. Although the production procedures are more or less the same, there are large differences between mustard types, explained as follows:

Mustard can be made from three different mustard corns or from a mix of mustard seeds. White mustard corns (Sinapis alba) are usually mild, black mustard (Brassica nigra) is very hot (it is used only rarely), and India mustard (Brassica juncea) is used very often. There are other variants as well.

There are different vinegar forms which define the taste of mustard. Apple vinegar, malt vinegar, spirit vinegar and other types are used. It is not necessarily vinegar that turns mustard flour in a paste. Grape must is used in some mustard forms. Each mustard mill adds spices, aromas, honey or spirits to the basic mustard mass according to individual taste or an old family recipe.

MUSTARD AND ITS FLAVORS

Sweet mustard: This mustard type is a mix of white and brown mustard corns which are milled coarsely, roasted slightly and sweetened with sugar or honey. The taste of the mustard is sweetish and is known as "Bavarian mustard." Traditionally, it goes very well with Weißwürsten and livercheese.

Mild mustard: This mustard is very popular and is called "select" or "table mustard." It is produced mainly from white mustard corns and its taste is delicately spicy.

Medium hot mustard: Also prepared from white and brown mustard corns, but is much hotter and children usually refuse to eat it.

Hot mustard: Produced mainly from brown corns. It is so hot that it will bring tears to your eyes.

Extra hot mustard: Extremely hot and is made mainly from brown mustard corns. If you eat a small portion, it burns your mouth and can unblock your nose if you have a cold.

GERMAN MUSTARD CULTURE

A. B. B. Mustard is the oldest mustard in Germany. In 1726, the Essers opened the first German mustard factory, which

was transferred to the possession of the Bergraths in 1781. In 1800, Adam Bernhard Bergrath took over the company and started printing his initials on white ceramic jars. Today, about 1,764 lbs (800 kg) of the mustard is sold in Düsseldorf per week. The mustard jars are often sold as souvenirs.

Mustard in East Germany: Bautzner mustard was almost unknown to West Germans and very popular with almost every East German. Besides this hot nostalgic product from Oberlausitz, you should taste Altenburg mustard from the skat town Altenburg near Leipzig if you have an opportunity. Niederfinower mustard from Uckermark has a nettle-flavor. In East Germany, people often preferred Czech mustard because it was more granulated.

Mustard in the south: Sweet mustard is made in Bavaria. A few years ago, you had to go south and cross the "Weißwurst equator" in order to buy this sweetish mustard specialty. A true Bavarian never eats Weißwürste without this sweet mustard.

FRENCH MUSTARD CULTURE

Dijon mustard: Although France has had a strong central government in Paris for the last couple centuries, culinary specialties are mostly developed outside of Paris. However, they have been enjoyed in the capital on a grand scale. Such is the case of mustard from Dijon, the capital of Burgundy, as well. Dijon mustard flour is not mixed with vinegar, but with juice from unripe grapes or must. Seed capsules are entirely or partially removed from its hot versions, giving the mustard a special piquancy.

The "Moutarde de Dijon" is available in three different, basic versions: mild, medium hot and extra hot. The mustard corns can be ground coarsely or finely and there are various herb flavors. Tarragon or green peppers are among the classics of the French mustard culture, but there are other types like Herbs de Provence, chives or champagne.

Bordeaux mustard: This mustard is mild and contains a higher share of seed capsules as well as at least 20 percent mustard powder. It is dark yellow, but it has a new red counterpart - Beaujolais mustard.

Rôtisseur mustard: Dark yellow, medium hot, coarsely ground mustard which contains a large share of mustard corns. Rôtisseur is a name of the job of "roast-cook" and does not refer to a town or a region.

ENGLISH AND AMERICAN MUSTARD CULTURE

On the British Islands, everything is always slightly different than on the continent. The British prefer mixing their own mustard. Therefore, mustard powder available

here is mixed with a little water. Besides their own particular powder, the British have their own mustard specialties as well.

English mustard: In contrast to continental mustard, English mustard is mostly made from brown mustard corns. The English top mustards are not produced with distilled vinegar, but contain mild malt vinegar. There are also differences in the degree of grinding the mustard corns. There are specialties like mustard with whisky, beer or mint.

American mustard: America reflects European mustard culture. Depending on the European origins of the settlers, the mustard is somewhat similar to English, French or German mustard. Yet American mustard has a unique characteristic: American mustard is refined with bourbon instead of whisky. American mustard seeds are used and their piquancy and flavor are adjusted to American taste buds.

DID YOU KNOW?
Since must is added to mustard, its name is *mustum ardens* originally, or 'spicy must' in English. The French *moutarde* and the English "mustard" originate from the Latin.

MEDICINAL USE: Mustard is a well-tested home remedy. A calf pack prepared with mustard is supposed to relieve cramps. Mustard dissolved in broth releases mucus and, as we know from experience, eating hot mustard unclogs your nose and clears the sinuses, helping you to breathe easier.

AROMATIC MUSTARD

Mustard with aromatic ingredients has existed as long as mustard itself. Herbal mustard and horseradish mustard are the classics. The choice of flavors keeps increasing: tomato, chili, poppy, pineapple, hot nettle and berry mustards are available.

TIPS FOR COOKING

You can marinate meat and fish with mustard. Mustard does not tolerate high temperatures for a long time or the essential oils contained in it evaporate. Therefore, always add mustard after cooking.

When preparing a salad dressing, always mix mustard with vinegar first and then add oil. Otherwise, it curdles fast.

IN THE KITCHEN

AROMA:
Depending on the ingredients, mustard can be mildly sweet or extremely hot. There are mustards with various spices, aroma and alcohol flavors.

USE:
Mustard is served with sausages, sauces, roast meat, poultry and cold cuts. Mustard goes well with mayonnaise and salad sauces. The taste of fish, herring and salmon particularly, is enhanced with mustard.

BUYING/STORING:
The mustard of Thomy, Hengstenberg, Kühne, Maille etc. is available in any supermarket. Mustard is available in jars and in tubes. Mustards from small regional mills are worth trying. Not all mustards are equal. You have only to visit a spice store in order to buy noble specialties. Even though mustard contains no preservatives, you can store it for up to 1 year. Opened mustard jars and tubes should be kept in the refridgerator.

Soy sauce and spicy sauces based on soy

Soy sauce

Origin:

Asia

Edible part:
Everything

Use:
✗

Property:
!

PRODUCTS: Japanese and Chinese Soy sauce

HISTORY: Soy sauces have a long history in Asian cuisine. Sources from the 6th century speak about a dark brown sauce similar to soy. Besides Chinese and Japanese soy sauce, every other Asian country has its own variation.

MANUFACTURING METHOD: Traditionally, soy sauce is prepared using natural methods in a process that takes several months. First, soy beans or a mix of soy beans are milled. The crushed soy beans or grains are mixed with mold (Aspagillus), water and salt, and the process of fermentation begins. Vegetable proteins are enzymatically decomposed, causing the brown color and spicy, full aroma characteristic of the sauce. Ideally, the mash ripens for several months or even a year. In order to save time and manufacturing costs, a process was introduced during which soy sauce is manufactured in only a few days. In this case, acid is added to the mash. The color, taste and

aroma of these fast manufactured soy sauces are caused by maize syrup, caramel coloring substances and artificial flavorings which must be specified on the package. You can, therefore, are easily distinguish a good, traditionally-produced soy sauce without any additives from an inferior sauce.

Chinese soy sauce

The original Chinese soy sauce is prepared purely from soy beans. There are two types: dark and light. The dark sauce can be stored longer than the light sauce and its taste is milder.

Japanese soy sauce

It is also called "shoyu" and was probably developed 1,000 years later than the Chinese soy sauce. It consists of only soy beans and wheat. In Japan, there are two types of soy sauce: light and dark. The light soy sauce is saltier but milder in taste. You cannot store it very long and Amazake, a sweet liquid, is added to it during the fermentation process.

Important warning:

High amounts of chloride propanol were identified in soy sauces in the past, usually in the non-traditionally prepared products. It is suspected that this substance is carcinogenic. Therefore, the European Commission laid down the legal maximum of 0.02 mg/kg and this value was binding in all European Union countries as of April 1, 2002.

In the kitchen

AROMA:
The taste of soy sauces is salty, spicy and, depending on the type, slightly sweet.

USE:
Soy sauce is the most important flavoring in Asian cuisine. It goes well with meat, fish, poultry and vegetarian dishes. In particular, it is suitable for marinating tofu, spicing sauces and soups and as a seasoning for the table. Soy sauce is a dip for sushi.

BUYING/STORING:
Soy sauce is available in supermarkets, Asian specialty stores or in delicatessens. It is available bottled. One cup bottles are preferable because soy sauce loses its aroma if stored open for a long time. Although storing the product in open bottles at room temperature does not harm the product, it is better to store soy sauce in the refridgerator.

TIPS FOR COOKING:
You can season both cold and hot dishes with soy sauce. Do not underestimate the salt content in soy sauce. Adding additional salt is usually not necessary.

Spicy, soy-based sauces

PRODUCTS: Bean sauce, Hoisin sauce, Teriyaki, Tamari, Ketjap Benteng, Miso

BEAN SAUCE
Bean sauce is a dark, thick sauce popular mainly in northern and western China and it contains fermented soy beans. There are two variations: mild and spicy variant, depending on the different spice and salt contents.

KETJAP BENTENG
Ketjap Benteng is an Indonesian soy sauce enhanced with spices, herbs and sugar. You can distinguish between slightly sweetened sauce with the addition of "asin" and intensely sweetened sauce with "manis."

HOISIN SAUCE
Hoisin sauce is a Chinese variant of soy sauce. It contains soy paste, garlic,

sesame oil, vinegar, chili and spices. It differs from other spicy sauces by its red color. It is served with Peking duck.

Teriyaki

Teriyaki is a special Japanese soy sauce. Additionally, teriyaki sauce contains wine, vinegar, sugar and Asian spices. It is ideal for grilling. Use it to marinate or rub on grilled meat. Owing to the sugar content, the meat caramelizes and turns an attractive color.

Tamari

Tamari is another type of soy sauce produced by lactic acid fermentation. It is a by-product of Miso production. Tamari is milder and usually less salty than normal soy sauce. It contains no wheat.

Miso

Miso is a brown paste made from soy beans and is very popular in Japan. It is used to prepare miso soup. Miso is dissolved in water and cooked with rice, vegetables and meat.

HAVE YOU EVER TASTED IT?

JAPANESE FONDUE
Cut 2 lbs beef in very thin slices and place on a tray. Prepare any of the following ingredients and place in small dishes: shiitake mushrooms, soy sprouts, bamboo sprouts, sliced water chestnuts, thinly sliced carrots, red peppers and green onions sliced in wide rings. Put ginger plums doused in honey, ginger doused in vinegar and soy sauce, chili sauce and miso sauce in separate dishes. Heat 1 quart chicken broth in a fondue pot. Each guest dips his morsel of meat, mushroom or vegetable in the broth or in choice of the sauces.

In the kitchen

Aroma:
All spicy sauces based on soy are salty, spicy or, depending on the particular type, sweet, hot or aromatic.

Use:
Soy sauces are used to spice all piquant dishes of Asian cuisine, whether to season grilled meat, sauces or soups, or to give individual ingredients an Asian flavor. Sauces based on soy go well with Asian rice and pasta dishes.

Buying/storing:
Spicy sauces based on soy are available in supermarkets, Asian specialty stores or in spice shops. Although they cannot spoil, try to buy them only in small bottles. The sauces lose their aroma once opened. They should be preferably stored in the refridgerator.

Tips for cooking:
Spicy sauces are used mainly to season hot dishes.
Do not underestimate the salt content and the piquancy of some of these spicy sauces and use them carefully because it is always possible to add more spices, but not vice versa.

Spicy sauces

Products: Worcestershire sauce, Maggi liquid spice, HP-sauce, A.1.-sauce, ketchup, salsa

WORCESTERSHIRE SAUCE

HISTORY: In 1835, Lord Sandys placed an order to two druggists, John Lea and William Perrins, to develop a sauce similar to the sauces which he enjoyed during his stay in India. When the druggists finished their sauces, they were not satisfied with the result, but forgot to get rid of the product. The discarded sauce lay in a barrel in a cellar for about 2 years until, by chance, they found it. Before they poured out the nostrum, they tasted the dark brown liquid and discovered, to their surprise, that it tasted slightly like spiced wine. Worcestershire sauce became a real hit shortly after

MANUFACTURING METHOD: Today Worcestershire sauce is not only manufactured by Lea & Perrins. The ingredients and the manufacturing method are similar, but not identical, in all Worcestershire sauces. The dark English spice is

prepared mainly from tamarind, chili, anchovies, malt vinegar, molasses, onion, garlic, sugar and a number of spices. Every producer keeps his formula secret. In order to produce a good flavor, the ingredients must be stored in wooden barrels for 3 years. During this period, the product matures and develops a spicy and sweetish aroma similar to sherry.

MAGGI LIQUID SPICE

HISTORY: In 1887, Julyus Maggi, a Swiss from Kempttal, developed Maggi spice. A German branch was established in "Gütterli-Hüsli" in Singen in the very same year. Originally, Julyus Maggi did not intend to produce a spicy sauce, but he spotted a magnificent business opportunity. Therefore, he started experimenting with legumes in 1882. In 1884, he introduced the first legume flour into the market and, 3 years later, a spice named after him. Although originally a product for poor people, you can find it in almost every German household, from multi-millionaires to the poor.

MANUFACTURING METHOD: The Maggi liquid spice consists of vegetable proteins, water, salt, aroma, glutamate and yeast extract. The vegetable protein decomposes during a fermentation process comparable with beer brewing, but no alcohol is produced. The spice matures for about 3 – 4 months in tanks, during which time it develops its characteristic aroma.

HP SAUCE

History: In 1899, a brown sauce called HP sauce was developed. The abbreviation "H.P." stands for "House of Parliament." The Gartons developed the formula. Mr. Garton first sold homemade sauce in his vegetable store in Nottingham before selling his formula to the producer of HP sauce.

Manufacturing method: HP sauce consists of a mix of malt vinegar, molasses, spirit vinegar, sugar, dates, tamarind, soy sauce, spices and salt. All the ingredients are mixed together and their combination results in the classic aroma of HP sauce. It contains no additives and is a purely vegetarian product.

A.1. SAUCE

History: This sauce was actually invented in London, although it is the most important grill sauce in North America today. The sauce is said to be invented by Henderson William Brand, chef of King George IV. The king was so excited about the sauce that he named it "A 1." The culinary success went to Brand's head and he founded a company producing essences and sauces. However, he lacked business skills and the company went bankrupt. W. H. Withall, his friend, saw potential in the product, took over the business in 1850 and managed it under the name Brand & Co.

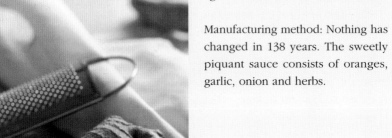

Manufacturing method: Nothing has changed in 138 years. The sweetly piquant sauce consists of oranges, garlic, onion and herbs.

KETCHUP

HISTORY: Ketchup, the red, thick, piquant and spicy sauce, is definitely the first sauce that children in the West encounter.

It is not absolutely clear who discovered ketchup. British sailors brought "ketsiap" or "kechap" from faraway Malaysia. The original sauce was a typical Asian fish sauce prepared from fermented fish, shells and spices. Richard Brigg, an English cook, is said to be the first person to come up with the idea to substitute the fish with tomatoes in 1792. Since then there has been tomato ketchup and, naturally, every company keeps its formula secret.

MANUFACTURING METHOD:

The basis of ketchup is tomato mixed with vinegar, sugar and spices like paprika, pepper, cloves, cinnamon, ginger, onion and nutmeg. Even though each company has its own formula, tomato ketchup must contain at least 7 percent tomatoes. Besides classic tomato ketchup, there are a number of variants. The most popular one is light brownish-yellow curry ketchup, but onion ketchup and Schaschlik ketchup can be found as well.

Salsa

History: We do not know for certain whether salsa was invented in Spain, South America or Mexico. However, one thing is sure: Spanish conquerors enjoyed the spicy sauces of the Indians and a sauce survived that is used mainly in Latin American cuisines even today.

Manufacturing method: Salsa is prepared from a mix of tomatoes, tomatillos, chili, onion, garlic and spices. In any case, the original salsa included cilantro. Depending on the particular type, it contains oregano, vinegar and oil as well. There are various degrees of piquancy ranging from "hot" or "medium" to "mild." The piquancy depends on the chili content.

Have you ever tasted it?

Tips for cooking
If you want to enhance dishes with these spicy sauces, add the sauces only after cooking or season with all these sauces individually at the table.
All these sauces contain salt. Therefore, more salt is probably unnecessary.

IN THE KITCHEN

AROMA:
All these sauces are spicy or extremely hot.

USE:
Worcestershire sauce is used to improve the taste of classic cuisine, particularly light sauces, ragouts, fish and egg dishes. A dash of Worcestershire sauce gives a Bloody Mary cocktail its proper taste. It is suitable for marinating grilled meat.

Maggi is a universal spice and goes well with all piquant dishes. It is great for livening up any insipid, lifeless dish.

HP and A.1. Sauces are classic grill sauces used as table spices in every good steakhouse and they complement meat and fish dishes as well as substantial stews.

Ketchup was actually developed as a grill sauce as well. However, it is used as a universal spice with pasta, eggs, potatoes and all savory dishes.

Salsa is the most piquant spicy sauce and is served with meat and fish dishes in Latin American cuisines.

BUYING/STORING:
All these sauces have a best-before date. Make note of it and always keep them in the refridgerator.

WHICH SPICE GOES WITH WHICH DISH?

Dish	Ajowan	Anise	Annatto	Devil's dung	Wild garlic	Basil	Wormwood	Comfrey	Sermountain	Fenugreek	Savory	Cayenne pepper	Chili	Curry leaf	Tarragon	Fennel	Galangal	Cloves	Ginger	Kaffir lime leaves
Egg												●			●					
Bread		●								●						●			●	
Baked goods		●																●	●	
Dessert		●																●	●	●
Seafood			●									●	●				●			
Fish			●				●			●		●		●	●	●	●	●		
Game											●							●		
Poultry	●		●	●			●			●	●	●	●	●	●		●	●	●	●
Lamb			●				●		●	●	●	●	●	●				●	●	●
Pork			●				●			●	●	●	●	●				●	●	●
Veal												●		●						●
Beef								●				●	●	●					●	●
Rice	●		●									●						●		
Pasta					●	●						●	●							
Potatoes											●	●								
Legumes	●										●			●						
Vegetables	●	●		●	●	●	●	●	●	●	●	●	●	●	●	●	●	●		
Salads					●	●		●								●				
Sauces					●	●	●					●	●	●	●			●		●
Soups				●	●	●	●	●	●			●	●	●	●	●		●	●	●

GOOD COMBINATIONS OF SPICES

Capers	Cardamom	Cassia	Garlic	Coriander	Cumin	Caraway	Turmeric	Bay leaf	Mace	Marjoram	Horseradish	Poppy	Nutmeg	Oregano	Paprika	Pepper	Allspice	Rosemary	Saffron	
●							●		●				●		●	●				Egg
				●	●	●						●			●					Bread
	●	●		●		●			●			●	●			●	●		●	Baked goods
	●	●							●			●	●			●			●	Dessert
			●				●		●				●		●	●				Seafood
●	●		●				●	●	●		●		●		●	●	●		●	Fish
			●						●				●		●	●	●	●		Game
	●	●	●	●	●		●	●	●	●			●	●	●	●		●	●	Poultry
	●		●		●	●		●		●			●		●	●		●	●	Lamb
	●		●	●		●		●		●			●	●	●	●		●		Pork
●	●	●		●					●		●		●			●		●		Veal
●	●	●	●	●				●	●		●		●	●	●	●	●	●		Beef
	●	●		●	●		●		●						●	●			●	Rice
			●				●						●	●		●			●	Pasta
				●		●		●		●			●	●	●	●		●		Potatoes
					●	●	●	●		●				●		●		●		Legumes
	●		●	●	●	●	●	●	●				●	●	●	●		●	●	Vegetables
●			●											●	●	●				Salads
●	●	●	●	●	●		●	●	●				●	●	●	●			●	Sauces
●	●	●	●	●	●	●	●	●	●	●	●	●	●	●	●	●			●	Soups

WHICH SPICE GOES WITH WHICH DISH?

	Sage	Salt	Sassafras	Chinese chives	Black cumin	Wild celery	Mustard	Sesame	Sezchuan pepper	Chinese anis	Sumac	Cicely	Tamarind	Thyme	Vanilla	Juniper	Wasabi	Common rue	Cinnamon	Lemon grass
Egg		●			●												●			
Bread		●			●	●		●												
Baked goods		●						●		●		●			●				●	
Dessert		●						●		●		●			●				●	●
Seafood		●	●											●	●					
Fish	●	●	●		●	●	●	●	●		●			●	●	●	●	●		●
Game		●						●						●		●				
Poultry	●	●	●		●			●	●	●	●		●	●	●		●		●	●
Lamb		●			●						●		●	●		●				
Pork		●			●			●	●	●				●	●	●		●		
Veal	●	●			●										●			●	●	●
Beef		●			●		●	●						●		●	●	●	●	
Rice		●									●		●						●	●
Pasta	●	●						●												
Potatoes		●			●			●	●					●						
Legumes		●			●						●	●	●					●		
Vegetables		●	●	●	●	●	●	●			●		●	●		●			●	●
Salads		●		●	●						●							●		
Sauces		●	●	●			●						●	●					●	●
Soups		●	●			●	●	●	●	●				●					●	●

GOOD COMBINATIONS OF SPICES

	Anise	Basil	Cayenne pepper	Tarragon	Cloves	Cardamom	Caraway	Bay leaf	Marjoram	Nutmeg	Oregano	Paprika	Pepper	Rosemary	Sage	Chinese anis	Thyme	Vanilla	Juniper	Cinnamon
Anise	●				●	●				●						●		●		●
Basil		●	●					●			●	●	●	●			●			
Cayenne pepper		●	●								●	●	●				●			
Tarragon				●				●				●	●	●			●		●	
Cloves	●				●	●		●		●						●				●
Cardamom	●				●	●				●						●				●
Caraway							●	●												
Bay leaf		●		●	●		●	●	●	●	●	●	●	●	●		●		●	
Marjoram								●	●				●				●		●	
Nutmeg	●				●	●		●		●			●					●		●
Oregano		●	●					●			●	●	●	●			●		●	
Paprika		●	●	●				●				●	●	●			●		●	
Pepper		●	●	●				●	●	●	●	●	●	●	●		●		●	
Rosemary		●		●				●		●		●	●	●	●		●		●	
Sage								●					●	●	●		●		●	
Chinese anis	●				●	●										●		●		●
Thyme		●	●	●				●	●		●	●	●	●	●		●		●	
Vanilla	●									●						●		●		●
Juniper				●				●	●		●	●	●	●	●		●		●	
Cinnamon	●				●	●				●						●		●		●

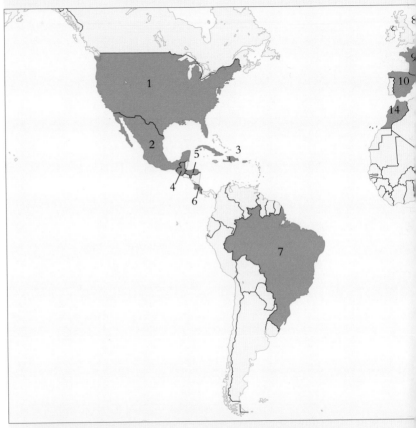

Map of the world of the countries producing spices

1 The United States: chili
2 Mexico: chili, paprika, vanilla
3 Antilles: chili, paprika, cinnamon, allspice, vanilla
4 Guatemala: cardamom, cinnamon, allspice, vanilla
5 Honduras: cinnamon, allspice
6 Costa Rica: cinnamon, allspice
7 Brazil: paprika, nutmeg, pepper, ginger
8 The Netherlands: caraway

9 France: chili, paprika, caraway
10 Spain: chili, paprika, saffron
11 Poland: caraway
12 Hungary: paprika, caraway
13 Mediterranean region: chili, saffron
14 Morocco: chili, caraway, cumin, saffron
15 Nigeria: ginger
16 Egypt: cumin
17 Tanzania: cloves
18 Comoros: cloves, vanilla

Map **295**

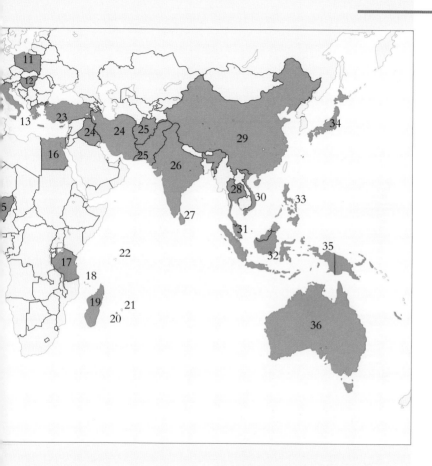

19 Madagascar: cinnamon, nutmeg, cloves,
   vanilla
20 Reunion: cloves, vanilla
21 Mauritius: nutmeg
22 Seychelles: cinnamon
23 western Asia: caraway
24 Iraq/Iran: saffron
25 Afghanistan/Pakistan: cumin
26 India: chili, caraway, cumin, cardamom,
   saffron, pepper, ginger
27 Sri Lanka: cardamom, cinnamon

28 Thailand: chili
29 China: chili, saffron, Chinese anis, Sezchuan
   pepper, ginger
30 Vietnam: Chinese anis, Sezchuan pepper
31 Malaysia: cardamom, pepper
32 Indonesia: chili, cinnamon, nutmeg, pepper,
   cloves, ginger
33 Philippines: Chinese anis
34 Japan: Chinese anis, ginger
35 New Guinea: nutmeg
36 Australia: ginger

INDEX - LIST OF SPICES

LIST OF RECIPES AND SPICE MIXES